e

Baedeker's

FLORENCE

Imprint

Cover picture: A view of Florence and it's cathedral

84 colour photographs
16 plans, 1 coat of arms, 1 special plan, 1 large city map

Conception and editorial work:
Redaktionsbüro Harenberg, Schwerte
English language: Alec Court

Text:
Linda and Heinz-Joachim Fischer, Rome
Revision and continuation: Baedeker Editorial Department

General direction:
Dr Peter Baumgarten, Baedeker Stuttgart
English translation: Babel Translations, Norwich

Cartography:
Gert Oberländer, Munich
Hallwag AG, Bern (city map)

Sources of illustrations:
dpa (29), Historia-Photo (9), Italian State Tourist Office (22), Prenzel (2), Rogge (22), ZEFA (1)

Following the tradition established by Karl Baedeker in 1844, sights of particular interest and hotels of outstanding quality are distinguished by either one or two asterisks.

To make it easier to locate the principal places listed in the "A to Z" section of the Guide, their coordinates on the large map of Florence are shown in red at the head of each entry.

Only a selection of hotels, restaurants and shops can be given: no reflection is implied, therefore, on establishments not included.

In a time of rapid change it is difficult to ensure that all information given is entirely accurate and up to date, and the possibility of error can never be entirely eliminated. Although the publishers can accept no responsibility for inaccuracies and omissions, they are always grateful for corrections and suggestions for improvement.

4th edition

© Baedeker Stuttgart
Original German edition

© 1990 Jarrold and Sons Ltd
English language edition worldwide

© 1990 The Automobile Association
United Kingdom and Ireland

US and Canadian edition
Prentice Hall Press

Licensed user:
Mairs Geographischer Verlag GmbH & Co. KG, Ostfildern-Kemnat bei Stuttgart

Reproductions:
Golz Repro-Service GmbH, Ludwigsburg

The name *Baedeker* is a registered trademark

Printed in Italy by G. Canale & C. S.p.A. - Turin

0 7495 0048 4 UK
0–13–369505–0 US & Canada

Contents

Preface

This Pocket Guide to Florence is one of the new generation of Baedeker city guides.

Baedeker pocket guides, illustrated throughout in color, are designed to meet the needs of the modern traveler. They are quick and easy to consult, with the principal sights of interest described in alphabetical order and practical details about location, opening times, etc., shown in the margin.

Each guide is divided into three parts. The first part gives a general account of the city, its history, notable personalities and so on; in the second part the principal sights are described; and the third part contains a variety of practical information designed to help visitors to find their way about and make the most of their stay.

The new guides are abundantly illustrated and contain numbers of newly drawn plans. At the back of the book is a large city map, and each entry in the main part of the guide gives the coordinates of the square on the map in which the particular feature can be located. Users of this guide, therefore, will have no difficulty in finding what they want to see.

Facts and Figures

General

Florence is the main city of Tuscany, the central Italian region, and one of Italy's 20 "regioni". It is also the chief town of the Province of Florence. The city certainly deserves the epithet "la bella" (the beautiful one). Its picturesque situation and a marvellous wealth of art treasures make Florence one of the most rewarding places in the world to visit.

Located on latitude 43°46'N and longitude 11°16'E, its altitude ranges from 160 ft (49 m) to 230 ft (70 m) on both banks of the Arno, amid a fertile basin surrounded by the Apenines and the hilly Tuscan landscape – altitude 160 ft (49 m)–230 ft (70m).

The city has 430,000 inhabitants and covers an area of 40 sq. miles (102 sq. km). **Area and population**

The Roman settlement of Florentia, which was established in 59 B.C., was almost square in shape. It stood on the right bank of the Arno and its northern border was on a line with where the Cathedral stands today, while the SW corner almost touched on the river. As the city boundaries gradually extended outwards under Byzantine rule in the 8th, 9th and 12th c. the left bank of the Arno also came to be part of the city. It was surrounded by a wall, sections of which can still be seen. Today the city is extending upstream towards the east, but new industrial development is located principally in the north-west.

In the Middle Ages Florence was divided into four Quartieri (quarters), named after the city gates – San Piero, Duomo or Vescovo, San Pancragio and Santa Maria. **Districts**
It was subsequently divided in six "Sestieri" (San Piero, Duomo, San Pancrazio, San Piero a Scheraggio, Borgo, Oltrano).
Nowadays Florence is divided into Quartieri, most of which are named after churches, including Santa Maria Novella, San Giovanni, Santa Croce, San Domenico and Santo Spirito. There are also the suburbs along the main trunk roads and on the hills of San Miniato, Belvedere and Bellosguardo in the S and Careggi, Montughi, Fiesole and Settignano in the N.

The Comune di Firenze are administered from the Palazzo Vecchio – which is the name chosen by the city authorities in preference to the more common Palazzo "della Signoria" or "Ducale". Communal elections are held every five years. **Administration**
Subdivision into smaller administrative units is still in its early stages.

Population and Religion

The city's rise from the Colonia Florentia of the Roman veterans to the flourishing Florence of the Renaissance was a slow process. About 1300 the city had c. 30,000 inhabitants. By 1348 **Population**

◀ *View of Florence and its Cathedral*

the number had risen to some 120,000 but only a third of the population survived the dreadful Plague of that year and the figure fell to 40,000.

The population figures did not reach 150,000 until the middle of the 19th c., since when they have continued to grow steadily.

Religion

99% of the Florentines are Roman Catholic. The city is the seat of an Archbishop, whom the Pope traditionally elevates to the rank of Cardinal.

The city does have churches for other religious denominations as well as a synagogue.

Transport

Airport

Through Galileo Galilei Airport at Pisa, 53 miles (85 km) away, Florence has good national connections with other major Italian cities.

The airport of Florence is Peretola, 3 miles (5 km) NW, which is served regularly by Alitalia and some other major airlines, but it can not be used by large aircraft.

Rail and buses

Florence is an important junction for rail traffic in central Italy. All intercity trains converge on Santa Maria Novella, the main station.

Buses cater for local transport within the city.

Motorways and trunkroads

Florence was already an important trading post on the Via Cassia during the Roman Empire and it built upon its position in the Middle Ages. Today the city enjoys excellent communications thanks to superhighways, expressways and well-engineered trunk roads.

The city lies on the Autostrada del Sole, the motorway from Milan to Reggio di Calabria, and is also connected by superhighway with Siena, Lucca, Pisa, Livorno and Genoa.

There are trunk roads to Bologna, Pontassieve (Forlì and Arezzo), Siena, Empoli and Prato (Pistoia and Bologna).

Culture

Since the Renaissance Florence has retained its standing as a center for art and culture. It has lost few of the churches and palaces, squares and bridges, frescoes and paintings which stem from the centuries when, in cultural terms, Florence was in its heyday. Since that time the city has been a magnet not only for tourists but also, and to an extraordinary degree, artists, art historians, and those engaged in restoration and historical sciences. Universities and institutes of scientific research, theaters and libraries, opera and concerts, all testify to the fact that the spirit of Florence lives on.

Universities and libraries

In addition to the state university, which has existed since 1349, but which was founded as a college in 1924, Florence has the following colleges: Università di Parigi, Università Europea, Università Internazionale dell'Arte, Università Libera per Attori. Nine public libraries are at the disposal of scholars and the general public.

People of Florence

With its buildings, churches, palaces and museums Florence offers unique opportunities for artistic and historical studies, which is why there are numerous academies (see Practical Information) and institutes concerned with science and culture. These include the Accademia della Crusca per la Lingua Italiana for the promotion of the Italian language, as well as various scientific institutes under the auspices of other nationalities.

Academies and other agencies

Twelve theaters, headed by the Teatro Comunale, meet the demand for modern plays, classic drama and opera.

Theaters and concerts

11

Florence has also won acclaim for its concerts, especially the offerings of the Maggio Musicale Fiorentina, the city's "musical month of May" which actually extends from May until the end of July.

Commerce and Industry

International status

Since the Middle Ages the Florentines, as industrious craftsmen, astute businessmen and good civic administrators, have always made sure that they prosper. At a time when Florentine bankers dominated the European money market they influenced the course of European politics. The ruling family of Florence, the Medici, owed their rise to the success of their trading and banking enterprises.

After Florence failed to match the political power of the other Italian states – the Republic of Venice, Dukedom of Milan, the Vatican State and the Kingdom of Naples and Sicily – it lost its ranking in commercial terms and as a consequence today is not a prominent international centre for commerce or banking.

Traditional industries

Towards the end of the Middle Ages the Florentines owed their wealth to the textile industry (weaving, dyeing, garment making and the silk trade) and in its present form of the clothing industry this is still an important income sector. Its artistic traditions have been retained in the highly developed craft sector (earthenware, china, embroidery, leatherware and basketry). Most jobs are to be found in chemicals and pharmaceuticals, precision engineering, the antiques trade, printing and publishing.

Many of the agricultural products of Tuscany are also processed in Florence.

Service industries

The commercial sector is nowadays of the highest importance for the city. Innumerable banks have their head offices here, its fashion fairs ("Alta Moda") are world famous, and its furs and antiques attract visitors from home and abroad.

Also allied to this is the importance of tourism – there is a constant flow of visitors throughout the year and at vacation periods, especially at Christmas, Easter and during the summer, Florence is always full to capacity.

Since, as chief town for the Region of Tuscany and the Province of Florence, the city is also the seat of regional and local government, the services sector as a whole plays an important part in the city's economy.

Prominent Figures in Florentine History

Cosimo de' Medici the Elder was so impressed by the paintings of Fra Giovanni, a Dominican friar in the convent at Fiesole, that he brought him to the Florence convent of San Marco which the pious monk then adorned with a series of frescoes and panels, mostly as aids to contemplation, in the cells of the friars, depicting scenes from the lives of Christ, Mary and the saints. As a result San Marco became the world-famous museum that can be seen today. Fra Angelico's works attest to a profound faith; his gentle Madonnas are imbued with an almost supernatural radiance which is why, and possibly also because of his angel-like saintliness, he became known as "Fra Angelico" or "Beato Angelico". The principal colors of his paintings, red, blue and gold, conveying sublimity and holiness, are reminiscent of medieval Gothic but his artistic forms anticipate the stylistic methods of the Renaissance. His grave is in Rome in the church of Santa Maria sopra Minerva.

Fra Angelico
(Fra Giovanni da Fiesole)
c. 1400–18.2.1455

The painter Botticelli, who spent virtually all his life in Florence and whose real name was Allessandro di Mariano Filipepi, is considered the foremost Florentine master of the early Renaissance. Most of his early works (Madonnas, portraits) were commissions for the Medici. He became famous mainly for his allegorical ("La Primavera" in the Uffizi), mythological ("Birth of Venus" in the Uffizi) and religious (Madonnas) portrayals of women. His pictures exhibit a fascinating sensuality which may be why he burnt some of his own paintings when urged to atone by the Dominican monk Girolamo Savonarola.
In 1480 Pope Sixtus IV summoned Botticelli to Rome where together with others he painted some of the frescoes for the walls of the Sistine Chapel.
Botticelli was also responsible for 94 pen and ink drawings in Dante's "Divine Comedy".

Sandro Botticelli
(Alessandro di Mariano Filipepi)
1444/1445–17.5.1510

Filippo Brunelleschi, born in Florence, was the first Renaissance architect and one of the greatest. He was the first to evolve the laws of linear perspective and his adherence to a perspective framework is seen at its best in his greatest feat of architecture, the dome of the Cathedral of Santa Maria del Fiore. The most important buildings in Florence for which Brunelleschi was responsible are the Spedale degli Innocenti, the churches of San Lorenzo and Santo Spirito, and the Pazzi Chapel.
As a sculptor he entered his relief "The Sacrifice of Isaac" (1402–3) in the competition for the second bronze door of the Baptistry which was won by Ghiberti. Brunelleschi's entry can be seen today in the Museo Nazionale del Bargello.
His monument with a bust by Buggiano is in the Cathedral.

Filippo Brunelleschi
1377–1446

A true Renaissance figure of tremendous vitality and accomplishment, the Florentine sculptor and goldsmith Benvenuto Cellini made an impact on his contemporaries through the

Benvenuto Cellini
(3.11.1500–14.2.1571)

Prominent Figures in Florentine History

Sandro Botticelli

Filippo Brunelleschi

Cosimo I de' Medici

artistic merit of his work no less than through his adventurous life which he described in his famous biography.

In Florence his ability as a sculptor can be admired in his "Perseus with the Head of Medusa" (completed 1554) in the Loggia dei Lanzi and in the bust of Cosimo de' Medici in the Museo Nazionale del Bargello.

The most famous example of his work as a goldsmith, and probably the only one still extant, is the salt-cellar made for François I of France in the Museum of Art in Vienna.

Cimabue
(Giovanni Cenni di Pepo)
c. 1240–after 1302

Little is known of Cimabue, the "Father of Florentine Painting", whose real name was Giovanni Cenni di Pepo. He was active in Rome (1272) and in Pisa (1301–2), where he is thought to have been engaged on a very poorly preserved St John in the cathedral. At the end of the 13th c. he was working in Assisi (frescoes in the Upper Church of San Francesco) and Florence where the majestic and forceful Santa Trinità Madonna in the Uffizi is generally attributed to him. It is thought that he may well have been the teacher of Giotto and he was acclaimed by Dante as one of the most highly renowned painters of his time.

Cosimo il Vecchio
de' Medici
(Cosimo the Elder;
27.9.1389–1.8.1464)

Cosimo il Vecchio (i.e. Cosimo the Elder) was the first and the greatest of the Florentine Medici family to rule the city, serving the best interests of its citizens and contributing to the embellishment of Florence. Its people, inspired by ancient Rome, entitled him "Pater patriae", father of the fatherland. Jacopo da Pontormo's expressive posthumous painting of him in the Uffizi portrays Cosimo as an astute man, conscientious and musical, by no means handsome but with an engaging mentality.

The son of Giovanni Bicci, a successful banker and elected Gonfaloniere, Cosimo, together with his brother Giovanni, was already at the age of 31 acting on behalf of his family's diverse interests. He was banished in 1433 following one of the many power struggles among the noble families for the political reins of the city. He returned to Florence a year later, to the people's jubilation, and was elected Gonfaloniere, an office which he held until his death.

In addition to his political activities, Cosimo the Elder in his merchant capacity extended his banking business throughout

Europe. As a patron he was generous in his advancement of artists, entrusting the building of the Palazzo Medici to the architect Michelozzo, and transforming the convent of San Marco where he founded the library and set to work the painters Fra Angelico and Fra Filippo Lippi. He founded the collection in the Medici Library (Biblioteca Laurenziana) and the School of Philosophy where Marsilio Ficino taught.

Cosimo lived at the time of the Council of Florence (1439–43) which gave him an insight into ecclesiastical and European politics. At his death he left behind a well-ordered city state and was deeply mourned by its people.

It was thanks to Cosimo I, Duke of Florence from 1537 and Grand Duke of Tuscany, upon his appointment by Pope Pius IV, from 1569, that the Medici family regained a position of political power in Florence.

Cosimo I de' Medici
(11.6.1519–21.4.1574)

Cosimo's father, Giovanni delle Bande Nere – so called because of the black armour he wore at the head of his Black Bands of mounted soldiers – had squandered large sums of money with his constant military ventures. At 17 Cosimo made his entry into the political life of Florence and by tyrannical means brought the city under his rule. Once this was assured he set about revitalizing its dormant economy and again made Florence a political power to be reckoned with.

As Duke of Florence he moved out of his family's townhouse, the Palazzo Medici, and into the Palazzo della Signoria which now became known as the Palazzo Ducale. Later he settled in the Palazzo Pitti, which became the political, artistic and intellectual hub of Florence, for Cosimo, a true Medici, was also patron to the artists of his time.

Successful though he may have been as a princely ruler, he did not enjoy the same measure of success in his private life. Seven of his eight children met with premature or cruel deaths.

Cosimo died in 1574, at the age of 55, after having handed over the affairs of state three years earlier to his son Francesco.

Dante Alighieri, Italy's greatest poet, was exiled from his native city.

Dante Alighieri
(May 1265–14.9.1321)

The son of a respected patrician family, Dante received his education from the Franciscans and Dominicans. He studied medieval philosophy, was interested in art and favoured a life of chivalry.

Florence was vouchsafed several years of peaceful prosperity after the reconciliation in 1279 of the warring Guelphs and Ghibellines, the parties of Pope and Emperor. When the hostilities recommenced Dante became embroiled on the side of the losing party which led to his banishment, on pain of death, from Florence. He was forced to live the rest of his life in exile and died in 1321 in Ravenna.

Yet Dante was haunted by two Florentine encounters. One of these was with Beatrice, the young girl he had known in childhood and whom, after her premature death, he passionately idealised in his poems; the other was with the city itself, at first loved by Dante and then hated and despised as "a city of shopkeepers". In his "Divine Comedy", the 3 by 33 cantos on Hell, Purgatory and Heaven, which came to be the prevailing concepts in the Western world of that time, Dante glorified Beatrice (thus ensuring her immortality) and passed judgement on the city of Florence and its citizens.

Prominent Figures in Florentine History

Donatello
(Donatello di Niccolò di Betto Bardi; c. 1386–13.12.1466)

Not only the greatest Florentine sculptor before Michelangelo, Donatello also ranks as the most influential individual sculptor of the 15th c., unsurpassed by any other in terms of heroic expression, multiplicity of themes and range of creativity. Apprenticed to Ghiberti, he then worked with Nanni di Banco. In his native city of Florence he was responsible for sculpting statues on the façade, outer walls and Campanile of the Cathedral as well as for the church of Orsanmichele.

His study of the classical remains in Rome then led him far beyond the bounds of medieval artistic sensibilities and capacities. With his bronze David (c. 1430, in the Museo Nazionale del Bargello) he created the first free-standing nude of the Renaissance, the bronze Gattemalata monument in Padua is its first equestrian statue, and Judith and Holofernes (1440), inside the Palazzo Vecchio, its first free-standing monumental group. Also outstanding are the Tabernacle with the Annunciation (c. 1434) in the church of Santa Croce and the Cantoria with dancing children for the Cathedral (1433–40, in the Museo dell'Opera del Duomo). His carved wooden Magdalene for the Baptistery (c. 1455, now also in the Cathedral Museum) exemplifies his ability as a sculptor to match beauty with ugliness and was crucial in the development of Florentine painting. The Medici honoured the sculptor by assenting to his interment in the crypt of Cosimo il Vecchio in San Lorenzo.

Lorenzo Ghiberti
(1378–1.12.1455)

Lorenzo Ghiberti achieved undying fame through the two bronze doors which he made for the Baptistry (Battistero San Giovanni) in Florence. It was as a painter that he entered the competition for the North Door, which he won. He devoted 21 year's work, from 1403 to 1424, to these doors but his greatest masterpiece was to be the East pair of doors, the "Porta del Paradiso", which he rightly inscribed "mira arte fabricatum" – "made with admirable art".

The scenes on the doors from the Old and New Testament, framed by saints, fathers of the Church and ornamentation, display Ghiberti's expressive capability as an artist, and his technical craft as a sculptor. Distinguished by their harmony of form and balance of movement, they signify his ability to link the Gothic expression of piety with the antique ideal of beauty of the Renaissance.

His three figures for the church of Orsanmichele are the first large bronzes of the new era in art.

Ghiberti was also an architect (collaboration on Florence Cathedral), goldsmith (unfortunately no work extant) and author (commentaries on Italian art of the 13th c., including his Autobiography).

In his workshops Ghiberti also employed other artists, including Michelozzo and Donatello.

Ghirlandaio
(Domenico di Tommaso Bigordi; 1449–11.1.1494)

Although Ghirlandaio's principal claim to fame is that Michelangelo Buonarroti was his apprentice, he was also the best fresco executant of his generation in Florence and responsible for typical examples of renaissance art: lively groups of his fellow Florentines against a landscape or an architectural background in confident perspective.

Ghirlandaio's principal works are six frescoes in the church of Santa Trinità, depicting scenes from the life of St Francis (1485) and frescoes of the lives of Mary and John the Baptist in the choir of Santa Maria Novella.

Dante Alighieri   *Leonardo da Vinci*   *Lorenzo de' Medici*

In his later paintings the collaboration of his pupils becomes progressively more evident.

The most famous sculptor in Florence after the death of Michelangelo, Giovanni da Bologna, known in Italy as Giambologna, was born in Flanders. He came to Italy in 1550, first to Rome then to Florence where he chose to settle and entered the service of the Medici in 1556.

Giovanni da Bologna (Giambologna; 1529–13.8.1608)

In 1579 this original and adventurous artist wrote to Ottavio Farnese that he was not so much concerned with the content of his work as with constantly testing his ability to shape a figure or a group with the greatest possible ingenuity and intensity of expression.

His sculptures in bronze and marble can be seen at many sites in Florence: the Piazza della Signoria (equestrian statue of Cosimo I de' Medici), in the convent of San Marco (reclining bronze figure in the Sacristy), in the Palazzio Vecchio, in the Loggia dei Lanzi (Rape of the Sabines), in the Giardino di Boboli of the Palazzo Pitti (statue of Abundance) and in the Museo Nazionale del Bargello (inter alia "Winged Mercury").

The name of Giotto di Bondone as architect is inexorably linked with the Campanile, the belfry of Florence Cathedral (Duomo Santa Maria del Fiore).

Giotto di Bondone (c. 1266–8.1.1337)

As an artist Giotto, together with Cimabue, is generally regarded as the founder of modern painting since, also influenced by French Gothic, he broke away from dependence on the stereotyped formality of Byzantine iconography.

Giotto's style of painting is based directly on the principle of direct observation of nature and reality, achieving a fresh approach to the stories of the Bible and the legends of the saints. His frescoes in the church of Santa Croce of scenes from the lives of St John the Baptist, St John the Evangelist and St Francis, his Ognissanti Madonna in the Uffizi and the frescoes in the Arena Chapel, Padua, are world-famous.

The Italian Renaissance brought a host of versatile personalities to the fore but it was only the genius of Leonardo da Vinci that brought together the skills of painter, sculptor, architect, natural scientist and engineer. He was comparable only with Michelangelo (they disliked one another intensely!) He was

Leonardo da Vinci (15.4.1452–2.5.1519)

17

the consummate artist of the Renaissance; his findings and research in the technical sphere demonstrate his universality of spirit.

Leonardo da Vinci was a pupil of Verrocchio and in 1472, at the age of 20, was already a Master in the Florentine Guild of Painters (first large-scale work of his own "Adoration of the Magi" in the Uffizi). From 1482 to 1498 he worked at the court of Duke Lodovico Sforza in Milan ("Virgin of the Rocks" and "Last Supper" in the refectory of the convent of Santa Maria delle Grazie, badly damaged). He worked in Florence again from 1500 to 1506, then in Milan and finally, from 1513 to 1516, in Rome. In 1517 he moved to France at the invitation of King François I.

The work carried out in the last twenty years of his life has almost all been lost or survives only in the form of copies by his pupils. The "Mona Lisa", probably his most famous painting, is in the Louvre in Paris, together with "Madonna and Child with St Anne". He started a wall-painting of the Battle of Anghiari for the Palazzo Vecchio in Florence but all but a section of the cartoon has been lost and nothing remains of the painting. The original scale model for a bronze equestrian monument of Duke Francesco Sforza was destroyed.

Leonardo was the architect of fortresses, devoted himself to intensely scientific projects, dissected corpses, wrote and illustrated an essay on the anatomy of the human body, projected aircraft and helicopters, made observations on the flight of birds, investigated the laws governing the movement of air and water and conducted botanical and geological studies. His many drawings, studies of movement in the human body, research into natural science, designs for buildings and technical projects attest to the catholicity of this Renaissance genius.

Lorenzo de' Medici
(Lorenzo the Magnificent;
1.1.1449–8.4.1492)

Lorenzo de' Medici was a typical Renaissance prince in his attitudes, education, patronage and style of government.

Lorenzo made use of the Medici banking funds and the backing of the people of Florence to raise the city to a position of cultural and political prominence in Italy. His brother Giuliano fell victim to the Pazzi conspiracy in the Cathedral in 1478 when Lorenzo, wounded, managed to take refuge in the sacristy. After the Pazzi affair the constitution was changed so that power was concentrated in his hands. A patron of the Platonic Academy, he was himself a talented poet. In the Medici Garden near San Marco he assembled a collection of Classical sculpture, brought the sculptors of his time together and was responsible for talented young men such as Michelangelo getting their training. Work was carried out on his behalf by Andrea del Verrocchio (Putto and Dolphin in the Cortile of the Palazzo Vecchio), Ghirlandaio and Sandro Botticelli. When Lorenzo died from a mysterious illness at the age of 43 Niccolò Machiavelli wrote: "Never perished in Italy a man famed for such great astuteness nor was a man's death such a great sorrow for his fatherland. Every fellow citizen mourns his death, not one forebore to manifest his grief at this event."

Lorenzo was originally interred in the old sacristy of San Lorenzo then subsequently laid to rest with his brother in the new sacristy designed by Michelangelo.

Niccolò Machiavelli

Michelangelo Buonarroti

Raphael

Niccolò Machiavelli, the great chronicler of Florentine history, is also the much maligned philosopher of man's struggle for power.

Niccolò Machiavelli
(3.5.1469–22.6.1527)

After the Medici were driven out of Florence in 1494 Machiavelli was secretary to the executive Council of Ten and therefore directly involved in the government of the Republic. He was often employed as an envoy on missions abroad. The Medici returned in 1512 and resumed power in Florence. From that time onwards Machiavelli withdrew to dedicate himself to literary pursuits, a watchful and astute observer of the political scene.

His major works are his discourses on the first ten books of Livy in which he expounds, through examples from Roman history, his ideas about the power of the State and the vicissitudes of history, and his most famous work "Il Principe" ("The Prince") which he completed in 1513 (not published until 1532) and in which he elaborated the political doctrine, the "Machiavellism" that entered into Western political thought, that the end justifies the means, however reprehensible, if it is for the good of the State.

Michelangelo Buonarroti, painter, sculptor, architect and poet, brought the art of the Renaissance to the peak of perfection.

Michelangelo Buonarroti
(6.3.1475–18.2.1564)

In 1488, at the age of 13, Michelangelo was apprenticed to the Florentine painter Domenico Ghirlandaio. Besides his aptitude for painting he increasingly developed his passionate interest in sculpture. In 1489 the young Michelangelo transferred to the school for sculptors set up in the Medici Garden. He left Florence in 1494 (before the expulsion of the Medici and the ensuing political upheaval when the Dominican monk Savanarola seized power) and, after a brief sojourn in Venice, worked in Bologna. He returned to Florence (1495–6) then journeyed to Rome where he stayed from 1496 until 1501. His "Bacchus" (Museo Nazionale del Bargello) and the Pietà for St Peter's in Rome date from this period.

Michelangelo was back in Florence from 1501 to 1505, when he created his "David" (Galleria dell'Accademia), the Bruges Madonna, the "Madonna Pitti" tondo (Bargello) and the painting "The Holy Family" (Galleria degli Uffizi). Because of his restless spirit, the years between 1505 and 1534 were spent zwandering between Florence, Rome and Bologna to work on commissions. During these years his achievements included the frescoes on the ceiling of the Sistine Chapel in the Vatican, the funerary chapel for the Medici in San Lorenzo in Florence, "Moses" for the tomb of Julius in Rome, the Boboli Slaves (Accademia), "Apollo" (Bargello) and "Vittoria" (Palazzo Vecchio). From 1534 until his death in 1564, apart from brief interludes, Michelangelo lived in Rome ("Last Judgment" on the altar wall of the Sistine Chapel in the Vatican, bust of Brutus in the Bargello, figures for the tomb of Julius in Rome, Projects for the Biblioteca Laurenziana at San Marco in Florence, and, in Rome, the Piazza del Campidoglio and, his greatest architectural achievement, the dome of St Peter's). The work of his old age, the marble group of the Pietà in Florence Cathedral (Opera del Duomo) and a few lines of his verse manifest the suffering of this great artist:

"Released of the burden that I groaning bore,
At last set free from all earthly desires,
A frail barque, to Thee, O Lord, I steer my course
From storm-tossed seas to Thy calm still waters."

Michelangelo's body was brought from Rome and laid to rest in the church of Santa Croce.

Raphael
(Raffaello Santi;
1483–6.4.1520)

Raphael, whose real name was Raffaello Santi or Sanzio, was the artist whose paintings most clearly and comprehensively represented the High Renaissance at its apogee, especially his Madonnas and his frescoes for the Vatican "The School of Athens" and the "Disputa".

Born in Urbino, the son of the painter Giovanni Santi, he became a pupil of Perugino in Perugia at the age of 17. In 1504 he moved to Florence where he set about learning all he could from the works of past and contemporary artists. After 1508 he lived in Rome where he succeeded Bramante (d. 1514) as architect of the new St Peter's. His twelve years in Rome were marked by his greatest artistic achievement, the Stanze de Raffaello frescoes in the Vatican.

Raphael's numerous paintings to be seen in Florence include: Pope Leo X with two Cardinals, Pope Julius II, Madonna with the Goldfinch and Portrait of Perugino in the Uffizi (Galleria degli Uffizi) and La Donna Velata, La Donna Gravida, Madonna del Granduca, Madonna della seggiola, Baldachin Madonna and Madonna dell'impannata in the Palazzo Pitti.

Raphael died at the age of 37 and was the only artist to be accorded the honor of burial in the Pantheon in Rome.

History of Florence

The Romans found Florentia near the former Etruscan settlement of Fiesole.	*c.* 300 B.C.
Florentia becomes a veterans' colony under Julius Caesar.	59 B.C.
The Ostrogoths under Radagasius lay siege to Florence but are beaten off by Stilicho.	A.D. 406
The Byzantine General Belisarius defeats the Ostrogoths under Totila.	539–41
The Lombards rule Northern Italy which is nominally part of the Eastern Roman Empire. They found the Duchy of Tuscia.	from 568
Charlemagne overthrows Desiderius, the Lombard King, and makes Tuscia a Frankish Margraviate.	774
Gerhard, a Cluniac reformer, becomes Bishop of Florence.	1045
Gerhard of Florence is installed as Pope Nicholas II.	1059
Matilda, Countess of Tuscia, mediates at Canossa in the investiture dispute between the Emperor Henry IV and Pope Gregory VII.	1077
Matilda abandons her role as mediator in the investiture dispute and wills her estates other than Florence, Lucca and Siena (i.e. the Matildan inheritance) to the Pope. Florence through siding with Matilda becomes one of the main allies of the Pope in the struggle against non-clerical influences.	*c.* 1079
Matilda grants Florence autonomous rights as a city.	1115
Florence destroys its neighboring rival city Fiesole.	1125
Under the rule of the nobility Florence has risen to the position of the leading power in Tuscany.	*c.* 1200
Emperor Frederick II conquers the Lombard league and the Pope excommunicates him. Frequent manifestations of the antagonism between the Ghibellines, the party of the Empire, and the Guelphs, the faction of the Church.	1237
The first Council of Lyons declares that Frederick II is deposed. Besides the factional disputes of the Guelphs and the Ghibellines Florence is riven by serious social strife between the nobility and the guilds of merchants and craftsmen.	1245
The Guelphs flee from the city.	1248
The Guelphs win the upper hand prior to the death of Frederick II. The imperial officials are dismissed and the guilds promulgate their own constitution, ushering in the era of "il Primo Popolo", the First Democracy.	1250

1252	Florence begins minting a gold ducat called the Fiorino or Florenus. This becomes current throughout Europe (hence the name "florin" for the Dutch guilder and the two-shilling coin in Britain).
1255	The Palazzo Pubblico is built to house the city's first democratic government.
1282	The new democratic constitution strengthens the "greater guilds" (arti maggiori) of the merchants against the "lesser guilds" (arti miniori) of the artisans.
1284	The third city wall is built to form an encircling defensive system but serves mainly to demonstrate political power.
1293	The Gonfaloniere (banner-bearer of Justice) replaces the Podestà (executive) and is meant to safeguard the interests of the commoners against the nobility. The chief authority is the Signoria under the direction of the Gonfaloniere.
1294	Start of building work on the Cathedral Santa Maria del Fiore.
1299	Building of the Palazzo Vecchio.
1302	The Guelphs banish the Ghibellines (including Dante) from Florence.
1333	The Arno floods and destroys many bridges and buildings.
1334	Pope Benedict XIII forbids the use of the names Ghibelline and Guelph under pain of banishment.
1340	First great Plague.
1347–8	Famine and a second plague epidemic reduce the Florentine population by one third.
1348	Vieri de Cambio de' Medici founds the first historically recorded Medici Bank.
1378	The revolt of the "Ciompi", an uprising led by the woolworkers, briefly achieves greater democratisation.
from 1405	Through the purchase (1405) and subjection (1406) of Pisa Florence achieves greater supremacy in Tuscany. The city is governed by an oligarchic junta headed by the Albizzi family.
1421	Florence gains access to the sea by acquiring the ports of Livorno and Portopisano and secures a prominent position in European trade. Giovanni di Bicci de' Medici becomes Gonfaloniere.
1433	Following defeat in the war against Lucca the Albizzi-dominated oligarchy place Cosimo the Elder under arrest and have him sentenced to ten years' banishment from the city.
1434	Rinaldo degli Albizzi falls from office and Cosimo de' Medici is recalled from exile to take his place as Gonfaloniere.
1444	Cosimo the Elder commissions the Palazzo Medici and founds the Medici Library (now Biblioteca Laurenziana).

Florence enjoys its greatest prosperity under Lorenzo the Magnificent (il Magnifico). The Medici Bank is weakened by mismanagement and lack of co-ordination.	1469–92
Two members of the Pazzi banking family, backed by Pope Sixtus IV, make an attempt on the lives of Giuliano and Lorenzo de' Medici. Lorenzo is wounded but survives. The conspirators are hanged. The constitution of Florence is redrafted on monarchic lines.	1478
The Dominican Friar and revivalist preacher Girolamo Savonarola calls on Florence to repent, announces the imminence of the Last Judgment and calls for reform of the Church.	1482
Savonarola elevates the convent of San Marco to a monastic congregation in its own right with a strict ascetic rule.	1493
Charles VIII of France invades Italy. Piero de' Medici, without consulting the Signoria, surrenders to him at Pisa. The Medici are driven out of Florence. Savonarola declares Christ the King of Florence and establishes a theocracy with statutes based on the Gospels.	1494
Savonarola is publicly executed by hanging and burning.	1498
As Gonfaloniere Piero Soderini carries out reforms and recaptures rebellious Pisa.	1502–12
Return of the Medici.	1512
Second expulsion of the Medici.	1527
Emperor Charles V makes the Medici Dukes of Florence.	1531
Conquest of Siena.	1559
Grand Duchy of Tuscany with Florence as chief town.	from 1569
Death of the last Medici. The Grand Duchy passes to the Austrian House of Lorraine.	1737
Florence becomes the capital of the new Kingdom of Italy.	1865–71
Republic of Italy.	1946
Florence suffers disastrous floods when the Arno bursts its banks. Countless dead and homeless and considerable damage to the historic fabric and art treasures of the city.	1966
In conjunction with the Council of Europe Italian institutions mount an exhibition on the theme of the Medici: "Florence and Tuscany of the Medici in Europe about 1500".	1980
Florence is named "European Cultural Metropolis" for one year.	1986
To counter noise and air pollution the use of private cars in the inner city is severely restricted.	1988

Quotations

Leondro Alberti
(1568)

"The city is very fair and rightly bears the name of Florence the Fair, the flower of Italy. There one sees magnificent buildings, some dedicated to God, some for the use of its citizens. One's gaze first falls upon the wondrous temple of Santa Maria del Fiore, all clad with marble, with the sublime cupola created by that most excellent Florentine, the architect Brunelleschi."

Jacob Burckhardt
(25.5.1818–8.8.1897)
Swiss art historian

"One finds united in the history of Florence the highest degree of political awareness and the greatest wealth of cultural forms, and in this sense the city may well have earned the title of the world's first modern state. Here it is an entire populace that engages in what is in the princely states a family affair. The wonderful Florentine spirit, at the same time artistic and acutely reasoning, unremittingly reshapes the political and social condition and describes and judges that same condition just as unremittingly. Thus Florence became the home of political doctrines and theories, of experiments and advances, but together with Venice the home of statistics and solely and above all other states in the world the home of historical image-making in the modern sense."

Cosmino the Elder
(Cosimo il Vecchio)
27.9.1389–1.8.1464

Guilding principle:
"Kingdoms fall through extravagance,
Cities rise through being austere.
See the Haughty, struck down by unseen hand."

Charles Dickens
(7.2.1812–9.6.1870)
English author
"Pictures from Italy"

"How much beauty is here, when, on a fair clear morning, we look, from the summit of a hill, on Florence! See where it lies before us in a sun-lighted valley, bright with the winding Arno, and shut in by swelling hills; its domes, and towers, and palaces, rising from the rich country in a glittering heap, and shining in the sun like gold!
Magnificently stern and sombre are the streets of beautiful Florence; and the strong old piles of building make such heaps of shadow, on the ground and in the river, that there is another and a different city of rich forms and fancies, always lying at our feet."

Max Frisch
(b.15.5.1911)
Swiss author

"In the chamber of Savonarola: the man is fascinating, the profile, next to it the small picture of his funeral pyre, the black face of the right-thinking, yet one must allow these judges something: they will soon be witnessing the execution, everything is ready on time, in its place, a wooden walkway leads from the court to the red flames. Here I sense something akin to my recent feelings at the Fishmarket: all the circumstances are public, on view in a human dimension, not anonymous."

"Florence is a manly town, and the cities of art that appeal to the current sensibility are feminine, like Venice and Siena. What irritates the modern tourist about Florence is that it makes no concession to the pleasure principle. It stands four-square and direct, with no air of mystery, no blandishments, no furbelows – no Gothic lace or baroque swirls ... The great sculptors and architects who stamped the outward city with its permanent image or style – Brunelleschi, Donatello, Michelangelo – were all bachelors. Monks, soldier-saints, prophets, hermits were the city's heroes. Saint John the Baptist, in his shaggy skins, feeding on locusts and honey, is the patron, and, except for the Madonna with her baby boy, women saints count for little in the Florentine iconography."

Mary McCarthy
(b.21.6.1912)
American writer "The Stones of Florence"

"The Italians say 'Firenze'. Compared with the English and French 'Florence' this has a hard, almost harsh sound. That is why d'Annunzio wanted people to use the old name, Fiorenza, which is what Dante called his native city. D'Annunzio's suggestion was not taken up, however. The sober, austere Florentines found the old name too rich, and, to a certain degree, too extravagant."

Eckart Peterich
(16.12.1900–13.4.1968)
German author

"The Cathedral, together with Campanile and Baptistery, is the most magnificent building in the city and I first turned my step in its direction after I had gazed my fill upon the Piazza del Gran Duca with its impressive Loggia dei Lanzi and many colossal statues, including those by Giovanni da Bologna of which I had become particularly fond. The Campanile adorned with fine multi-colored marble exerts an immediate charm and surpasses in reality any image of it that I have ever seen. It is clear from the very first glimpse that its creator was an artist rather than a builder for it is color that predominates among the elements brought together to such charming effect."

Max Nohl
Italian Sketchbook
(1805)

"Apart from some Dutch cities, Florence is probably the cleanest city in the world and certainly one of the most elegant. Its neo-Gothic architecture possesses all the purity and perfection of a lovely miniature. Fortunately for the beauty of the city, its citizens, when they lost their freedom, also lost the energy to embark on large buildings. In consequence nowhere here is the eye affronted by an ignoble façade and there is nothing to disturb the fair harmony of these streets which are imbued with the medieval ideal of beauty."

Stendhal
(23.1.1783–23.3.1842)
French writer

Florence from A to Z

Suggestions for sightseeing programmes in Florence will be found in the Practical Information Section on pages 140–176.

Note

Arciconfraternità della Misericordia

J5

("Archconfraternity of Mercy")

This Order, the oldest and most distinguished association of Florentine citizens for social and charitable purposes, was founded in 1326, when the Plague raged in Florence, to aid the sick poor and attend to their burial. Michelangelo was a member of the Order which used to wear red hoods (these are now black) and which has its headquarters near the Duomo Santa Maria del Fiore (see entry). The duties of the Order used to include accompanying condemned prisoners to the place of execution. Nowadays the confraternity runs a modern ambulance service and a first-aid centre. It has over 2000 members, all volunteers, and is funded by donations.

Location
Piazza del Duomo 19

Buses
B, 1, 4, 6, 7, 10, 11, 13r, 14, 17, 19r, 23, 25, 31, 32, 33

Arcispedale di Santa Maria Nuova (Hospital)

K5

Early in the 14th c. Florence's old hospital was considerably enlarged and renamed Santa Maria Nuova (St Mary the New). Most of the present spacious building between Via degli Alfani, Via della Pergola, Via Bufalini and Via Sant'Egidio dates from the 17th c. An interesting feature is the clearcut articulation of the loggias overlooking Piazza Santa Maria Nuova.

Location
Piazza di Santa Maria Nuova

Buses
13r, 14, 19r, 23, 31, 32, 33

*Badia Fiorentina (Church)

K6

The spire of the Badia opposite the Palazzo del Bargello (see entry) is an unmistakable feature of the skyline of Florence. This church of a Benedictine abbey was founded in 978 by Willa, the mother of Ugo, Margrave of Tuscany (commemorated here every year on 21 December, the anniversary of his death). The church was subsequently enlarged by Arnolfo di Cambio in the 13th c. and then internally virtually rebuilt in the Baroque style by Matteo Segaloni in the 17th c.
Interesting features of the Gothic façade are the portal by Benedetto da Rovezzano (1495) with a "Madonna and Child" (early 16th c.) in glazed terracotta by Benedetto Buglioni in the lunette.
A walk round the church should take in the following points of interest:

Location
Via del Proconsolo
(access from Via Dante Alighieri also)

Buses
13, 14, 19, 23, 31, 32

◄ *Badia Fiorentina and its distinctive church spire*

Filippino Lippi's masterpiece (1485) "The Madonna appearing to St. Bernard" (left of the entrance).
Tomb of Ugo, Margrave of Tuscany (d. 1001), built between 1469 and 1481 by Mino da Fiesole (in the left transept).
The beautiful 15th c. cloister, popularly known as the "Chiostro degli Aranci" because of its orange trees.

Battistero San Giovanni (Baptistery)   J5

Location
Piazza S. Giovanni

Buses
B, 1, 4, 6, 7, 10, 11, 14, 17, 19, 23, 25, 31, 32

The "Baptistery of St John" or, in Dante's words, "il bel San Giovanni", was completed about 1128, 70 years after building had commenced. It is famous for the three massive bronze doors on the S, N, and E sides and for the magnificent mosaics in its octagonal interior.
A number of builders were responsible for the construction of what, after 1128, was to serve as a baptistry. Its pleasing proportions and green and white marble scheme of decoration made it an architectural masterpiece that was to serve as a model for other European buildings. The three bronze portals – works of sculpture unsurpassed in the Western world – were added in the 15th c.

S portal

The S portal is the oldest and was designed by Andrea Pisano (1318–30) and cast by Leonardo d'Avanzano (1330–8). It is divided into 28 square Gothic panels. With workmanship reminiscent of the art of the goldsmith, the reliefs on 20 of the panels depict scenes from the life of John the Baptist, patron saint of the church; the other eight panels are allegorical representations of the theological and cardinal virtues. Every figure stands out in clear relief, each one a unique work of art in the modelling of the face, of the folds of the garments and the expressive posture of the body.
The decorations of the framing are by Vittorio Ghiberti, son of Lorenzo, and their foliage, creatures and fruit are an early indication of the wealth of form that characterised the Renaissance.

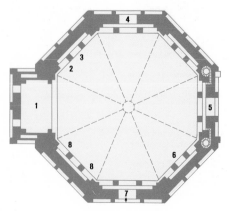

Battistero San Giovanni

1 Tribuna (high altar) with mosaics by Jacopo

2 Sarcophagus of Bishop Ranieri

3 Tomb of the Antipope John XXIII

4 N door

5 E door (Porta del Paradiso)

6 Marble font

7 S door (entrance)

8 Roman sarcophagi

In 1401 Lorenzo Ghiberti beat six others (including Brunelleschi and Jacopo della Quercia) to win the competition for the N portal. From 1403 to 1424 Ghiberti worked on the bronze doors with his assistants (Masolino, Donatello, Paolo Uccello, Bernardo Ciuffagni, Bernardo Cennini) and in doing so adhered closely to Andrea Pisano's design for the S portal: 28 square panels each with a Gothic relief, twenty of them scenes of the Life of Christ and eight of them the figures of the four Evangelists and four Early Fathers of the Latin Church. His work, however, far excels that of Pisano in the grace of the figures and the liveliness of expression. Ghiberti's difference of approach, while still keeping to the traditional forms, is particularly evident in the vivid scenes of the "Resurrection" (right-hand door, top row, left), the "Baptism" and the "Temptation of Jesus" (left-hand door, 4th row down, left and right), the "Nativity" (left-hand door, 5th row down, right) and "Christ among the Doctors" (right-hand door, 5th row down, right).

Ghiberti also designed the bronze framing of the portal from which small heads protrude at every intersection.

N portal

Ghiberti adopted an entirely new approach when he came to design his greatest work, the E portal. Michelangelo considered it worthy to serve as the Gate of Paradise (hence the name "Porta del Paradiso") and Ghiberti himself sang its praises by adding "mira arte fabricatum" ("made with admirable art") on the right-hand door next to his signature.

E portal

N door   *S door*   *E door*

Nowhere else has a sculptor expressed himself in bronze as perfectly as in this door, created between 1425 and 1452. The ten separate panels contain reliefs of scriptural subjects. The framing incorporates figures of prophets and sibyls and portrait medallions, including one of Ghiberti himself (4th from the top in the middle row on the left).

The beauty and mastery of the finely delineated perspectives, the three-dimensional levels of representation, the individual characterisation of the figures, the meaningful composition of the groupings, all combine in the consummate perfection of the whole.

From top left to bottom right the panels depict the following:

Adam and Eve: creation, fall, expulsion from the Garden.

Cain and Abel: sacrifice of Cain and Abel, death of Abel, punishment of Cain.

Noah: his sacrifice, departure from the Ark, his drunkenness.

Abraham and Isaac: angel appearing to Abraham, Isaac's sacrifice.

Jacob and Esau: birth of Esau and Jacob, selling the birthright, Esau hunting, Rebecca, Isaac's betrayal.

Joseph: selling of Joseph, Benjamin, Joseph and his brothers.

Moses: Moses receiving the Tablets of the Law on Mount Sinai.

Joshua: the Jews before Jericho, encampment, the walls come tumbling down at the sound of the trumpets.

Saul and David: Saul in battle against the Philistines, slaying of Goliath.

Solomon and the Queen of Sheba.

This door rightly has the place of honour opposite the Duomo Santa Maria del Fiore (see entry).

Porta del Paradiso: Moses receiving the Tablets of the Law on Mount Sinai

The sombre, mystical nature of the dim interior of the Baptistry comes as something of a surprise after the clearcut articulation of the exterior. It is dominated by the octagonal dome (diameter 84 ft – 25·6 m) which is completely lined with mosaics, the work of Florentine artists (Jacopo da Torrita, Cimabue, Andrea di Riccio, Gaddo Gaddi) in the 13th c. or possibly about 1300 and therefore at the time of Dante. One of the greatest mosaics in the Western world, it is as outstanding for its treatment of its subject matter as for the richness of its ornamentation.

In the centre is the gigantic figure of Christ as Judge of the World at the Last Judgment. Grouped around him, in different sections, are the figures of the Resurrected and the Damned, of angels, apostles, prophets and saints, with Mary and John the Baptist ranged against the realm of the Devil, devourer of men. (It should be recalled that Dante, Italy's greatest poet, who in his "Divine Comedy" describes Heaven, Purgatory and Hell, came from Florence.) Other vivid mosaics depict the "Creation of the World", scenes from the life of Joseph and of Jesus Christ, Mary and John the Baptist.

Also of interest are one of Donatello's masterpieces, the tomb of the Antipope John XXIII (deposed by the Council of Constance) and the niello decoration of the marble floor (zodiac and ornamentation), the marble font, the sarcophagus of Bishop Ranieri and the high altar with a candlestick in the form of an angel.

Another of Donatello's masterpieces used to stand in the Baptistry – his wooden statue of Mary Magdalene – but this is now in the Museo dell'Opera del Duomo (see entry).

Biblioteca Mediceo-Laurenziana

See San Lorenzo

Biblioteca Nazionale Centrale (National Library)   K6

The large building of the National Library (built 1911–35) on Corso dei Tintori, Via Magliabechi and Piazza dei Cavalleggeri, near the Santa Croce complex (see entry), contains 24,721 manuscripts, 723,138 letters and documents, 3780 incunabula, over four million books, 5855 volumes and 4451 sheets of music, 630 atlases and 14,754 geographical and topographical maps.

Of especial value are an early 14th c. copy of Dante's "Divine Comedy" (probably the oldest in existence), manuscripts by Galileo, and missals and bibles dating from before the invention of printing. The library dates back to the 13th c. and preserves manuscripts by all the famous Florentines.

Location
Piazza dei Cavalleggeri

Buses
14, 19r, 23, 31, 32

Opening times
Mon.–Fri. 9 a.m.–7 p.m.
Sat. 9 a.m.–1 p.m.

Boboli Gardens

See Giardino di Boboli

Brancacci Chapel

See Santa Maria del Carmine

Campanile

See Duomo Santa Maria del Fiore

Cappelle Medicee

See San Lorenzo

Casa di Bianca Capello   H6

(House of Bianca Cappello; formerly the house of the Corbinelli)

Location
Via Maggio 26

Bianca Cappello was the daughter of a noble Venetian family and the sweetheart and later wife of Grand Duke Francesco I. Her house, which was completely rebuilt by Bernardo Buontalenti in 1567, is a fine example of the mansions lived in by the nobility of that time. It has an unusual feature in the grotesque representations of bats below the windows.

** Casa Buonarroti (Michelangelo House and Museum)   K/L6

Location
Via Ghibellina 70

Bus
14

Opening times
Mon., Wed.–Sun.
9.30 a.m.–1.30 p.m.

Closed
Tues.

Michelangelo bought the house for his nephew Leonardo di Buonarroti but never lived in it himself. Leonardo's son, Michelangelo, decorated it and turned it into a memorial to the great artist. It was completely restored in 1964.

Two original sculptures by Michelangelo merit special attention: "Battle of the Centaurs and Lapiths", a marble relief which, although Michelangelo was only 17 when he created it, presages in the sense of movement and substantial nature of the figures, much of his later mastery; and "Madonna of the Steps" ("Madonna della Scala"), Michelangelo's earliest work, completed at the age of 16. The signs of genius are already clearly marked in the sense of space, the flow and counterflow on the steps on the left (hence the name, "Madonna of the Steps"), the fineness of the profile, the fall of the mantle.

The wooden crucifix (1494) from Santo Spirito (see entry), supposedly Michelangelo's earliest work for a church, is also interesting. Christ is depicted not as a man of sorrows but as a gentle handsome youth.

Other items on display are models or copies of the works of Michelangelo or mementoes of the artist's life. There are also sculptures and paintings by other masters.

Casa e Museo di Dante (Dante's House and Museum)   J/K6

Location
Via Dante Alighieri 4

Buses
14, 19, 23, 31, 32, 33

The houses that belonged to the Alighieri family are in Via Dante Alighieri. According to Florentine tradition one of them was the birthplace in 1265 of one of Florence's greatest sons, the poet Dante Alighieri who did not exactly find favor with his native city. Dante opposed the attempts by Pope Boniface

Casa Buonarroti

Casa di Dante

VII to incorporate Florence and the whole of Tuscany into the Papal States. When Charles de Valois was summoned to Florence by the Pope to treat for peace, Dante, as leader of the Ghibellines, was exiled from the city.

The museum contains photographs, editions of the "Divine Comedy", reproductions of Botticelli's drawing for Dante's work and portraits of the greatest of the Italian poets.

Opening times
Mon., Tues., Thurs.–Sat.
9.30 a.m.–12.30 p.m.,
3.30–6.30 p.m.;
Sun. and public holidays
9.30 a.m.–12.30 p.m.

Closed
Wed.

Cascine   A3–F5

W of the town the Cascine park extends more than 2 miles (3 km) along the Arno. Formerly farms belonging to the Medici and subsequently the Lorena family, the park was opened to the public by the Grand Dukes of Lorraine in the second half of the 18th c.

Its large race-course is one of the park's main attractions.

Location
On N bank of Arno.

Buses
2, 9, 13r, 17, 26, 27

Casino di San Marco (Also Casino Mediceo)   K4

The palace on the site of the former Medici gardens was built by Bernardo Buontalenti in 1574 for Grand Duke Francesco I de' Medici who had his artist's studio and alchemist's laboratory here.

Today the building houses the Court of Appeal.

Location
Via Cavour 57

Buses
1, 6, 7, 10, 11, 17, 25

Cenacolo di Foligno (Foligno Refectory) J5

Location
Via Faenza 42

Buses
1, 19n, 28, 34

At present closed
for restoration

The refectory of the former convent of St Onuphrius, which belonged to the Franciscan nuns of Foligno, contains Perugino's "Last Supper". It was seriously damaged in the 1966 flood. With this work Perugino proved that he was the equal in Florence of Andrea del Castagno and Ghirlandaio.
At present closed for restoration.

Cenacolo di San Salvi (St Salvi Refectory) O6

Location
Via di San Salvi 16

Buses
3, 6, 14, 34

Opening times
Tues.–Sun. 9 a.m.–1 p.m.

Andrea del Sarto's masterpiece, his version of the "Last Supper" in the Cenacolo di San Salvi, is well worth seeing. It is one of the finest early 16th c. frescoes in Florence.
The gallery in front of the refectory and the refectory itself also contain other works by Florentine masters. The monastery kitchen with its huge fireplace is also worth a visit.

*Cenacolo di Sant'Apollonia (Refectory of Sant'Apollonia) J/K4/5

Location
Via XXVII Aprile 1

Buses
B, 1, 4, 6, 7, 10, 11, 17, 20, 25, 34

Opening times
Tues.–Sat. 9 a.m.–2 p.m.
Sun. and public holidays
9 a.m.–1 p.m.

Closed
Mon.

Admission is free

The former convent of Sant'Apollonia, which was secularised in 1808, then used as a military storehouse and which now houses part of the university, is worth visiting on account of its interesting church and the beautiful cloister with its graceful 15th c. columns.
The Coenaculum of St Apollonia, the convent's refectory, is now a museum.
The refectory of the Benedictine convent of Saint Apollonia, previously inaccessible because of the nun's seclusion, contains Andrea del Castagno's "Last Supper" (c. 1457). This fresco has an important place in Renaissance painting: the accuracy of its perspective and the realistic physical vigour of the figures (especially Jesus and the figure of Judas sitting apart from the others) make the picture intensely dramatic.
Also interesting are (above it) Castagno's "Crucifixion", "Entombment" and "Resurrection" and his two lunettes "Pietà" and "Christ crucified with the Virgin, St John and Saints".

*Certosa del Galluzzo (Carthusian Monastery)

Location
Galluzzo, 3 miles (5 km) S

Bus
41

The Carthusian monastery of Galluzzo is equally famed for its architecture and its works of art.
Niccolò Acciaiuoli, an important Florentine statesman and a friend of Petrarch and Boccaccio, had the monastery built in 1341 for the Carthusians, an anchorite order founded by St Bruno of Cologne. It contained blocks of individual cells for the

The Carthusian monastery of Certosa del Galluzzo

monks and common areas for prayers and services. In earlier days the monastery was richly endowed with art treasures, but Napoleon robbed the order of about 500 works of art and only a few were ever returned.

In two rooms of the art gallery there are examples of the once immense collection of art treasures on display, including four lunette frescoes of Christ's Passion by Pontormo (based on drawings by Dürer) and a "Madonna and Child" by Lucas Cranach.

The monastery buildings which, unlike those of other Orders, were not where the monks lived – their cells were in separate blocks – but where they assembled for communal activities include a parlatory, a medium-sized cloister, the chapter house, the "Great Cloister", the refectory, the "Small Cloister" and finally the pharmacy where the monastery's souvenirs and liqueurs are on sale.

In the late 18th and the early 19th c. Pope Pius VI and Pope Pius VII spent long periods in the Foresteria, the monastery's guest-house.

The church of San Lorenzo, which is worth seeing, is reached by crossing a large square. The Cappella di San Tobia (left of the high altar) contains the tomb of Niccolò Acciaiuoli and the tombstones of three other members of the Acciaiuoli family (including that of Lorenzo di Niccolò).

In the Cappella di Sant'Andrea is the famous tomb of Cardinal Agnolo II Acciaiuoli, formerly ascribed to Donatello but now thought to be by Francesco da Sangallo.

Opening times
Summer: Tues.–Sun.
9 a.m.–noon, 3–6 p.m.
Winter: Tues–Sun.
9 a.m.–noon, 2.30–5 p.m.

Closed
Mon.

San Lorenzo (church)

Chiostro dello Scalzo (Cloister of the Discalced) K4

Location
Via Cavour 69

Buses
1, 6, 7, 10, 11, 17, 25

Opening times
Tues.–Sat. 9 a.m.–2 p.m.
Sun. and public holidays
9 a.m.–1 p.m.

Closed Mon.

The Chiostro dello Scalzo, a graceful cloister with slender columns, was decorated by Andrea del Sarto between 1514 and 1526 for the "Confraternity of St John the Baptist", whose crossbearers used to walk barefoot (scalzo) in processions. The famous frescoes depicting scenes from the life of John the Baptist have been restored several times.
The most important frescoes, all monochrome, are the Birth of John the Baptist (1526), the Sermon of St John (1515) and the Dance of Salome (1522). Admission is free.

Colonna della Croce al Trebbio (Column) J5

Location
Via del Moro

Buses
6, 11, 36, 37

This granite column, which stands at the junction of Via del Moro, Via delle Belle Donne and Via del Trebbio, was erected in 1338. It has a fine Gothic capital, decorated with the symbols of the Evangelists, and a cross of the Pisan school.

Conservatorio Musicale Luigi Cherubini K5
(Museo degli Strumenti Musicali Antichi, collection of old musical instruments)

Location
Via degli Alfani 80

Buses
B, 1, 4, 6, 7, 10, 11, 17, 25

At present closed

The Conservatorio, founded in the early 19th c., houses a comprehensive music library and a collection of old musical instruments, including early pianos by the inventor of the pianoforte, Bartolomeo Cristofori, violins by the famous Italian violin-makers Stradivarius and Amati, and musical instruments from ancient Egypt and the Orient.
The collection was founded in the early 18th c. by Ferdinando, the son of Cosimo III. Cristofori was its curator and was also responsible for the most important acquisitions.

Dante Museum

See Casa e Museo di Dante

** Duomo Santa Maria del Fiore e Campanile J/K5
(Cathedral of Santa Maria del Fiore and Campanile)

Location
Piazza del Duomo

Buses
1, 6, 7, 10, 11, 13r, 14, 17,
19r, 23, 25, 31, 32, 33

Opening times
Mon.–Sat. 10.30 a.m.–5 p.m.

The cathedral of Florence is more than the symbol of the city. Together with the Campanile and the Baptistery (see Battistero) it forms one of the most magnificent works of art in the world. Florentines could not survive without a glimpse of the dome of their cathedral. It would seem that when Michelangelo was creating the dome of St Peter's he was seeking to transplant Brunelleschi's masterpiece from his native city of Florence to Rome.
At the end of the 13th c. the citizens of Florence, conscious of the growing importance of their city, wanted to erect a great new edifice on the site of the church of Santa Reparata that would surpass the other churches in the city in its beauty and

The dome of the cathedral – symbol of Florence

its dimensions. Famous architects, first Arnolfo di Cambio (from 1294), then Giotto, Andrea Pisano, Francesco Talenti and Giovanni Ghini made such progress with the building work despite numerous interruptions that between 1420 and 1434 Filippo Brunelleschi was able to crown it with the dome – that sensational feat of architectural bravura. In 1436 the cathedral was dedicated to St Mary the Virgin and acquired the epithet "del Fiore" from the lily on Florence's coat of arms.

The present ornate façade, designed by Emilio de Fabris', was not added until 1875–87. (The old façade, which had never been completed, was demolished in 1587.) The cathedral has some impressive dimensions. It is 526·28 ft (160·45 m) long; the nave is 141 ft (43 m) wide; the transept 298 ft (91 m) wide; the façade is 164 ft (50 m) high; the dome is 375·1 ft (114·36 m) high and 149·31 ft (45·52 m) in diameter. The church's 89,308 sq. ft (8300 sq. m) of floor space can take about 25,000 people. Santa Maria del Fiore is Italy's third largest church after St Peter's in Rome and Milan Cathedral.

The main feature of the exterior is the rich articulation with   Exterior colored marble – white from Carrara, green from Prato and red from the Maremma. There is marble everywhere – on the façade built in the medieval Gothic style, on the sides of the aisles leading to the nave, on the buttresses, the small side domes and the massive main dome.

Dome
In his building of the dome Brunelleschi gambled on creating a structural masterpiece (with modest wisdom he commended

37

it to the protection of the Virgin) which is both powerful and aesthetically pleasing. The white ribs that meet at the lantern clearly outline the contours of the red covering of the dome.

The streets behind the apse offer an impressive view of the mountain of marble that is the cathedral and Brunelleschi's dome. At this point there is a gallery on the drum of the dome. This was built at the time of Michelangelo who was intensely critical of it, voicing the opinion that it looked like a "cricket cage".

In the pavement in front of the apse is a marble slab marking the spot where on 17 January 1600 the gilded ball from the dome hit the ground and shattered after it had been struck by lightning. It was replaced by a larger one below the cross.

The lantern, too, was often a victim of lightning but was unremittingly repaired. Today it is protected by a modern lightning conductor. (Visitors may climb up inside the dome as far as the lantern; the stairs start from the left aisle.)

Sculpture

The exterior has an abundance of sculpted figures: on the top spandrel of the façade "God the Father", with, immediately below, busts of famous Florentine artists; under a huge rose window "Virgin and Child" and statues of the apostles; below that in the niches of the four pillars are bishops of Florence and Pope Eugene IV who consecrated the church in 1436. The bronze doors have reliefs of Mary and allegorical figures of the Christian virtues.

Portals

While walking round the cathedral it is well worth having a look at the four portals.

On the right-hand side near the Campanile:

Porta del Campanile, with "Christ giving a Blessing" in the gable and "Madonna and Child" in the lunette, both in the style of Andrea Pisano.

Porta dei Canonici. Above the "Porch of the Canons" is a "Virgin and Child" by Lorenzo di Giovanni d'Ambrogio.

Nearby are the memorials to the architects Arnolfo di Cambio and Brunelleschi and a stone with the inscription "Sasso di Dante" marking the spot where the poet is supposed to have watched the cathedral being built.

On the left side:

"Porta della Balla" (late 14th c.). The door has a polychrome "Madonna and Child and two Angels". The twisted columns at the sides are supported by lions.

"Porta della Mandorla." The finest portal in the church, this "Porch of the Glory" was designed by Giovanni d'Ambrogio and Nanni and completed by various artists (Donatello, Niccolò di Pietro Lamberti and Ghirlandaio). Above the door in the "almond" is the Virgin borne up by angels (1421, by Nanni di Banco); in the lunette is a mosaic of the "Annunciation" by Domenico and Davide Ghirlandaio (1491).

Interior of the church

Severity and beauty are also the theme of the interior of the cathedral which makes its impact through its Gothic forms, its soaring arches and pillars, untrammelled by gaudy ornamenta-

Elaborate decoration on the façade of the cathedral of Santa Maria del Fiore ▶

Duomo Santa Maria del Fiore e Campanile

E side of the cathedral

Fresco above the main door

tion to detract from the feeling of spaciousness (later additions were removed during restoration), while the sense of severity is heightened by the earthy hue of the stonework.

The ground plan of the cathedral is a Latin cross with a nave and two aisles; the space beneath the dome is enlarged by its extension into the three surrounding apses.

Despite its bare aspect, the interior has some rich and precious figures.

Front

The three stained-glass windows above the main portals depicting St Stephen (left), the Assumption of the Virgin (centre) and St Laurence (right) were designed by Lorenzo Ghiberti and executed by Niccolò di Piero.

Above the central door is a mosaic depicting the Coronation of the Virgin (c. 1300, by Gaddo Gaddi) together with the famous clock with hands that move anticlockwise. The heads of prophets in the corners were painted in by Paolo Uccello in 1443.

Right of the main portal is the Gothic tomb of Bishop Antonio d'Orso (d. 1321) by Tino da Camaino (incomplete; various parts in the Museo Nazionale del Bargello, see Palazzo del Bargello).

North aisle

In the first marble recess is a statue of Joshua (early 15th c.) by Bernardo Ciuffagni, Donatello and Nanni di Bartoli.

Opposite the second pillar is a fresco transferred on to canvas by Niccolò da Tolentino (1456).

Duomo Santa Maria del Fiore

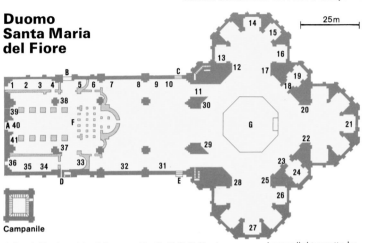

Campanile

A Portale Maggiore with relief "Maria in Gloria", by A. Passaglia

B Porta della Balla

C Porta della Mandorla, by Giovanni d'Ambrogio and Nanni. Above the portal, Nanni di Banco's Virgin borne up by angels

D Porta del Campanile with Annunciation

E Porta dei Canonici, above "Madonna col Bambino", by d'Ambrogio

F Cripta di Santa Reparata, remains of old cathedral

G Brunelleschi's dome with fresco of the Last Judgement by Vasari and precious stained-glass windows

1 Window "S. Stefano e due Angeli", by Ghiberti

2 Bust of Emilio de Fabis, designer of the façade, by V. Consani (1887)

3 Statue of Joshua (head by Donatello)

4 Bust of Arnolfo di Cambio, by U. Cambi (1843)

5 Bust of the organist Squarcialupi, by Benedetto da Maiano (1490)

6 Equestrian figure of Niccolò da Tolentino, painted by A. del Castagno (1456)

7 Equestrian figure of Giovanni Acuto (John Hawkwood), painted by P. Uccello (1436)

8 Window dated 1395. Below in the marble recess a statue of

King David (B. Ciuffagni, 1434)

9 "Santi Cosma e Damiano", by Bicci di Lorenzo (15th c.)

10 14th c. window, below, "Dante and the Divine Comedy", by D. di Michelino (1456)

11 Stairs up to the dome

12 "S. Tommaso", by De' Rossi, 16th c. statue

13 "S. Giuseppe", painting by Lorenzo di Credi

14 Marble altar (Buggiano)

15 "Madonna with Saints", altarcloth in the style of P. Bonaguida

16 "Pietà", by Michelangelo (now in cathedral museum)

17 "S. Andrea", by A. Ferrucci, statue (16th c.)

18 In the door lunette, "Risurrezione", terracotta, by Luca della Robbia (1444). Bronze door, also by della Robbia, assisted by Michelozzo and Maso di Bartolomeo

19 Sagrestia nuova o delle Messe

20 "S. Pietro", by B. Bandinelli, statue (16th c.)

21 Above the altar, two angels carrying candles (Luca della Robbia, 1450). Below the altar, reliquary of St Zenobius (Ghiberti, 1432–42)

22 "S. Giovanni", by B. da Rovezzano, statue (16th c.)

23 In the lunette, "Resurrection"

in enamelled terracotta, by Luca della Robbia (1450)

24 Sagrestia vecchia o dei canonici

25 "S. Giacomo Minore", by G. Bandini, 16th c. statue

26 Fragment of a fresco in the style of Giotto, "Madonna del Popolo"

27 Michelozzo's altar

28 "S. Filippo", by G. Bandini, 16th c. statue

29 "S. Matteo", by De' Rossi, 16th c. statue

30 "S. Giacomo Maggiore", by J. Sansovino, 16th c. statue

31 Bust of the philosopher Marsilio Ficino, by A. Ferrucci (1521)

32 In the marble recess, a statue of Isaiah, by B. Ciuffagni (1427)

33 "S. Bartolomeo in Trono," by R. di Jacopo Franchi

34 Roundel, by B. da Maiano, showing Giotto at work

35 Bust of Brunelleschi, by A. Cavalcanti

36 Window "S. Lorenzo e Angeli", by Ghiberti

37 Stairs down to the Cripta di Santa Reparata

38 Recess, with St Zanobius stamping out pride and cruelty, by G. del Biondo (late 14th c.)

39 Tomb of Antonio d'Orso

40 "L'Assunta", window, designed by Ghiberti

41 "Incoronazione di Maria", mosaic, by G. Gaddi

41

To the right of this is the equestrian figure of John Hawkwood (Giovanni Acuto in Italian), commander of the Florentine mercenary army, painted by Paolo Uccello (1436) to imitate sculpture.

In the next marble recess is the statue of King David made for the façade by Bernardo Ciuffagni (1434).

Below the window is a painting by Domenico di Michelino glorifying Dante (1465), a late rehabilitation of the poet by the city that once sent him into exile.

The staircase that leads up to the dome starts from the point where the aisle joins the apse. There is a marvellous panoramic view from the lantern.

North apse (or "Tribune")

The N apse is divided into five chapels. The stained-glass windows were designed by Ghiberti.

In the fourth chapel is an interesting double-sided retable in the style of Pacino di Bonguida depicting the "Madonna and Saints" and "Annunciation and Saints".

In the pavement is Toscanelli's gnomon which since 1468 has been used for astronomical calculations such as the summer solstice, indicted by the sun's rays which, on 21 June, shine down through a conical hole in the lantern of the dome precisely on to this metal plate.

Dome

On the inner surface of the dome (undergoing restoration) is the great fresco of the Last Judgement by Giorgio Vasari (begun in 1572 and completed by Frederico Zuccari in 1578). The stained glass in the round windows of the drum was executed from cartoons by Ghiberti, Paolo Uccello and Andrea del Castagno.

At the foot of the pillars supporting the drum are eight statues of apostles. Against the first pillar on the left stand St James the Greater by Jacopo Sansovino and St Thomas by Vincenzo de Rossi, and against the second pillar on the left stand St Andrew by Andrea Ferrucci and St Peter by Baccio Bandinelli. On the opposite side the third pillar on the right has St John by Benedetto da Rovezzano and St James the Less by Giovanni Bandini and against the fourth pillar on the right are St Philip, also by Giovanni Bandini, and Vincenzo de Rossi's St Matthew.

Choir

Under the dome is the choir with the high altar. The octagonal marble balustrade is based on a design by Baccio d'Agnolo; the 88 reliefs decorating it are by Baccio and Giovanni Bandinelli. The high altar (by Baccio Bandinelli) and the crucifix (by Benedetto da Maiano; 1495–7) are also of interest.

New Sacristy

The sacristies are especially interesting. In the lunette above the door of the new Sacristy is a glazed terracotta "Resurrection of Christ" by Luca della Robbia (1444).

The fine bronze door is also the work of Luca della Robbia (with Michelozzo). Its ten panels depict Mary with the Infant Jesus, John the Baptist, Evangelists and early Fathers.

This sacristy is where Lorenzo the Magnificent took refuge in 1478 when he and his brother were attacked during a service in the cathedral on the day of the Pazzi conspiracy. Lorenzo managed to escape but his brother Giuliano perished.

Central apse
In the Cappella di San Zenobio (Chapel of St Zenobius) in the central apse is a fine bronze urn by Lorenzo Ghiberti containing the relics of the saint.

Old Sacristy
Above the door of the Old Sacristy ("dei Canonici", "of the Canons") is a terracotta relief of the "Ascension of Christ" by Luca della Robbia. In the sacristy can be found a piscina by Buggiano, Lorenzo di Credi's "Archangel Michael" and two terracotta candlesticks in the form of angels, also by Luca della Robbia.

South apse (or "Tribune")
The S apse is also divided into five chapels.
The first chapel (after the Old Sacristy) contains an interesting fresco by Giotto: "Madonna del Popolo".
The details of the statues against the pillars supporting the drum are given in the section on the dome.

South aisle
Interesting features here include a bust below the window of Marsilio Ficino (1521), the great Renaissance philosopher, and a medallion depicting Giotto by Benedetto da Maiano (1490; opposite the last pillar).
Next to it in a wooden recess is the statue of the prophet Isaiah by Nanni di Banco (1408) and a medallion of Brunelleschi. This is the work of Andrea Cavalcanti, known as Buggiano, who was the heir and favorite pupil of Brunelleschi.
The door leading out to the Campanile is also in this aisle.
From the cathedral porch stairs lead down into the old Cathedral of Santa Reparata (4th/5th c.) and to the tomb of Brunelleschi.

Cripta di Santa Reparata

Campanile (bell-tower)

One of the great landmarks of Florence, the Campanile, the cathedral belfry, 269 ft (82 m) high and 47·6 ft (14·5 m) wide, was begun in 1334 by Giotto (di Bordone). After his death in 1337, Andrea Pisano continued the building of the belfry in accordance with Giotto's plans but his successor, Francesco Talenti, deviated from the original design. The tower was completed in 1387. It is well worth while climbing the 414 steps for the splendid view of the city from the top.
The building is characterised by the harmony of its dimensions, the strength of the octagonal pillars, the delicate articulation of the intervening walls and the intricate alternation of the colors of the marble.
On the lowest storey are two rows of panels containing allegorical bas-reliefs. Most of the hexagonal panels are by Andrea Pisano, who worked to Giotto's designs, and Luca della Robbia. They depict the life of Man, his work and his art.
The lozenge-shaped panels in the second row contain allegories of planets, virtues, liberal arts and sacraments.
The niches in the second storey above these lozenges used to contain statues of saints, prophets and sibyls sculpted between 1300 and 1400 by Florentine artists (including Donatello). Today these are kept in the Museo dell'Opera del Duomo (see entry). There are copies in some of the niches.

Opening times
Summer:
daily, 9 a.m.–7 p.m.
Winter:
daily, 9 a.m.–5 p.m.

*Fiesole

The little town of Fiesole, 968 ft (265 m) above the Arno, is an Etruscan foundation of 7th–6th c. B.C. Towards the end of the 1st c. B.C. the Roman town of Faesulae arose; it had a capitol, a forum, a temple, a theater and baths. However, during the time of the migration of the peoples the town declined and was later completely overshadowed by its neighbor Florence. Since 492 Fiesole has been the seat of a bishop.

An excursion to Fiesole should be undertaken, not only for the beautiful panoramic view of Florence from either of the hilltops of San Francesco and Sant' Apollinare, but also for the sights of the town itself.

Location
5 miles (8 km) NE

Bus
7

Piazza Mino da Fiesole

In the center of the town lies the broad Piazza Mino da Fiesole (named after the sculptor Mino da Fiesole, c. 1430–1484); this was the ancient forum, and on the north side stands the Cathedral, begun in 1028, extended in the 13th and 14th c. and considerably altered in the 19th c. The Duomo San Romolo has been an episcopal church since the 11th c.; its predecessor stood on the site of the present Badia Fiesolana. The battlemented campanile, more than 138 ft (42 m) high, dates from the 12th c.

The interior is notable for its frescoes and pictures, especially in the Cappella Salutati.

Cathedral

Fiesole

| 100 m |

Via Dupré · Via d. Mura Etrusche · Giardini · Teatro Romano · San Francesco · Pubblici · Piazza d. Mercato · Sant' Alessandro · Duomo · Piazza Mino da Fiesole · Piazza Garibaldi · V. Gramsci · San Girolamo · Vecchia Fiesolana · Via · Via · V. S. · Ansano · Verdi · Via S. Apollinare · Firenze

| 1 Palazzo Pretorio | 3 „L'Incontro di Teano" | 5 Palazzo Vescovile |
| 2 Santa Maria Primerana | 4 Museo Bandini | 6 Seminario |

◀ *Giotto's Campanile: the bell-tower of the cathedral*

45

Fiesole

Museo Bandini
(closed Sun.)

To the N of the cathedral is the Museo Bandini, containing a collection of religious works of art, including many pictures of saints, which Canon Angelo Maria Bandini, librarian of the Biblioteca Mediceo-Laurenziana (see entry) and scientist, had been assembling since 1795. After his death the collection passed to the Cathedral Chapter of Fiesole and is now in this museum.

Seminary Building
Bishop's Palace

On the narrower NW side of Piazza Mino da Fiesole stand the stately building of the Seminario, dating from 1697, and the Bishop's Palace (Palazzo Vescovile) which was an 11th c. foundation.

Palazzo Pretorio
Santa Maria Primerana

On the SW side of the square are two interesting buildings; the Palazzo Pretorio (14th and 15th c.), which is decorated with coats of arms, and the medieval Oritorio Santa Maria Primerana, with a 16th-c. portico.

Monument

The monument in the square is called "Incontro di Teano" (1906). The bronze equestrian statues represent Victor Emanuel II and Garibaldi.

Zona Archeologica (Excavations)

Theater

On the NE behind the Cathedral extends the excavation site, Zona Archeologica. The center of interest is the Roman theater, not discovered until the beginning of the 19th c.; it was built at the beginning of the imperial age (1st c. B.C.) and was extended under the emperors Claudius and Septimius Severus. The semi-circular amphitheater has a diameter of 111 ft (34 m) and has room for about 3000 spectators in 24 rows; the stage area measures 87 ft (26·4 m) by 21 ft (6·4 m).

Baths

Not far from the theater are the ruins of a Roman bathing establishment which was also constructed at the beginning of the imperial age and enlarged under the Emperor Hadrian. Although the arches, supported by huge pillars, were still visible, it was not realized until the end of the 19th c. that this was a Roman bathing establishment and the complex was then excavated.

Temple

In the NW corner of the site can be seen the remains of a Roman temple (1st c. B.C.) and also of an Etruscan temple (3rd c. B.C.).

Etruscan Wall

On the N the archeological site is bordered by a preserved part of the huge Etruscan town wall.

Museum
(closed Mon.)

In the little archeological museum, to the S of the Roman theater, artifacts of the Roman and Etruscan periods are exhibited; among them is a stele (470–460 B.C.) on which are representations of a funeral meal, dancing and fighting between animals, the head of the Emperor Claudius and a Dionysus statue (a Roman copy of a Greek original).

San Francesco

Giardini Pubblici

To the NW of the central square (Piazza Mino da Fiesole)

Fiesole: The Roman theater

extends the town park (giardini pubblici), from which there are extensive views.

On the W side of the park, at an altitude of 1132 ft (345 m), stands the monastic Church of San Francesco. It was built in the 14th c. and given over to the Franciscans in 1407. In 1905 the church was extensively restored.

Monastic Church

The interior with valuable art treasures, the mission museum and the idyllic cloisters are all worth seeing.

Mission Museum

San Alessandro

To the S of San Francesco stands the Church of Sant' Alessandro, probably founded as early as the 3rd c. A.D. It was originally called San Pietro in Gerusalemme but is now dedicated to Bishop Alexander of Fiesole. It occupies the site of an old Etruscan temple which was later replaced by a Roman temple of Bacchus. At the beginning of the 6th c. Theodoric the Great is said to have converted the building into a Christian church which in the course of time was refashioned on several occasions. There is a magnificent view from the terrace over the valley of Florence.

Church

Villa Medici

By following the Strada Vecchia Fiesolana, which leads SW downhill from Fiesole, one reaches the Villa Medici, also known as "Belcanto" or "Il Palagio di Fiesole"; it was built by the architect Michelozzo between 1458 and 1461 for Cosimo the Elder.

It was here that the Pazzi conspirators began to plan the murder of the brothers Lorenzo and Giuliano de' Medici, but they later found the Duomo Santa Maria dei Fiore (see entry) as more convenient (1478).

San Domenico di Fiesole

The hamlet of San Domenico di Fiesole (486 ft (148 m) above sea level) is situated a little more than half a mile (1 km) SW of Fiesole on the boundary of the City of Florence, of which there is a panoramic view. Notable here is the Church of San Domenico (1406–1435; rebuilt in the 17th c.) with a richly furnished interior. In the first chapel on the left can be seen a beautiful altarpiece by Fra Angelico (c. 1430).

Badia Fiesolana

To the NW below San Domenico, at an elevation of 404 ft (123 m), lies Badia Fiesolana, where until 1026 stood the cathedral church of Fiesole, now replaced by the present cathedral. After Camaldolese monks had rebuilt the church and monastery (badia=abbey), the buildings passed to the Benedictines. During the Renaissance the monastery and the church were again rebuilt; on the façade of the church can be seen Romanesque features, dating from the 12th c.

Since 1976 the international academic institute "Università Europea" has occupied Badia Fiesolana.

Forte (Fortezza) del Belvedere (Also Forte di San Giorgio) J7

Location
Costa di San Giorgio/Van San Leonardo

Buses
13, 38

The massive fort above Florence on the left bank of the Arno was the work of the architect Buontalenti (1590–5), probably based on plans drawn up by Giovanni de' Medici. It was commissioned by Grand Duke Ferdinando I who intended it to serve as a stronghold where he could safeguard his family and all their riches. Inside is a small palace, also designed by Buontalenti, which today is used for temporary exhibitions.

The ramparts of the star-shaped bastion near the Porta San Giorgio (see entry) afford a splendid view of the city.

Fortezza da Basso (Or di San Giovanni Battista) H/J4

Location
Viale Filippo Strozzi

Buses
1, 4, 7, 10, 14, 17, 19r, 22, 23, 25, 28, 31, 32, 33

The vast five-sided fortress near the main station, today used as a barracks, was designed in 1534 by Antonio Sangallo the Younger and built under the direction of Pier Francesco da Viterbo and Alessandro Vitelli (1534–5). With this bastion Alessandro de' Medici sought to manifest and consolidate his power after his return to the city.

Fountain of Neptune

See Piazza della Signoria

** Galleria dell'Accademia (Academy Art Gallery)   K5

The spacious rooms of the hospital of St Matthew near the former church of San Matteo house the "Academy", the Galleria dell'Accademia, founded in 1784 by Grand Duke Pietro Leopoldo I of Lorraine. Together with the other famous art galleries of Florence (in the Palazzo degli Uffizi and Palazzo Pitti – see entries), it houses tapestries and important paintings of the Florentine school from the 13th to 16th c.

Location
Via Ricasoli 60

Buses
B, 1, 4, 6, 7, 10, 11, 17, 25

Opening times
Tues.–Sat. 9 a.m.–2 p.m.,
Sun. and public holidays
9 a.m.–1 p.m.

Closed
Mon.

Many pictures are not yet in their final positions, but it should be possible to see the following:

Room 2: Early Renaissance works of the Florentine school.
Room 3: "Madonna" by Botticelli.
Room 5: Duccio's "Christ crucified" and "Tree of the Cross".
Room 6: "Madonna and Child with two Angels and four Saints" by Orcagna. "Trinity" by Nardo di Cione.
Room 7: "Coronation of the Virgin" by Jacopo di Cione, "Pietà" by Giovanni da Milano, scenes from the lives of Christ and St Francis by Taddeo Gaddi.

Works by Michelangelo
The Academy's main claim to fame is for its sculptures by Michelangelo, with his "David" taking pride of place. It was removed from its original location in the Piazza della Signoria (see entry) in 1873 and set up here to protect it from the ravages of the weather (traces of this are still visible). The statue in the Piazza is a copy.
At the age of 26 Michelangelo had accepted a huge block of marble which had been rejected by others because of its proportions – it was over 13 ft (4 m) high but not very "deep". He worked on it from 1501 to 1504 to produce a figure of youthful energy and beauty, his "David", who, according to the Bible, was an Israelite shepherd-boy who emerged victorious from his seemingly hopeless battle with the giant Goliath.
Even Michelangelo's contemporaries praised his statue's virtues: the perfect harmony of the body, the noble posture of the head, the alert and confident expression on the face, the tension of the warrior and the tranquillity of the future victor. The David became the symbol of the spirit of liberty in Florence, the irrepressible urge for independence of its citizens and their political body, the Signoria. During the disturbances in the city in 1527 (when the Medici were driven out) David's left arm was smashed but the fragments were gathered up and reassembled.
To the right of the David is a bronze portrait of Michelangelo by Daniele da Volterra, probably the most authentic of the known portraits of the artist.
The Accademia is the place where, in the uncompleted figures of the Slaves, St Matthew and Pietà di Palestrina, it is possible to follow most closely Michelangelo's creative process as a sculptor.

49

Galleria dell'Accademia: Michelangelo's "Slaves" and "David" (in the background)

Cavaliere Garden: Monkey Fountain

Fontana del Bacco

Michelangelo intended the "Slaves" for the tomb of Pope Julius II in Rome. He spent from 1519 to 1536 working on six statues but was unable to complete them. After his death they were set up in the Giardino di Boboli (see entry). Four of them are now in the Academy – the "Awakener", the "Bearded One", the "Young One" and the "Atlas" (the other two are in the Louvre in Paris).

Before 1505 Michelangelo sculpted St Matthew, one of the apostles planned for the tomb of Julius II. It was the only one of the twelve he even started and though not completed it is highly expressive. The finished parts of the statue blend into the unhewn sections of the marble to form a whole.

Galleria d'Arte Moderna (Gallery of Modern Art)

See Palazzo Pitti

Galleria Corsini

See Palazzo Corsini

Galleria Ferroni (Museum Ferroni)   J5

The collection of paintings in this gallery was presented to the city in 1850 by Marchese Ferroni. At present they are in store, because some of the 15th–18th c. paintings are in need of restoration. Eventually they are to be put on show again. The gallery is situated near the Church of Sant' Onotrio (patron saint of smiths) di Foligno. In the nearby refectory of the former nunnery can be seen Perugino's "Last Supper", which was damaged in the flood of 1966.

Location
Via Faenza 40–48

Buses
1, 19, 28, 34

Galleria Palatina or Pitti

See Palazzo Pitti

Galleria degli Uffizi (Collection of paintings)

See Palazzo degli Uffizi

* Giardino di Boboli (Boboli Gardens)   H/J7

Behind the Palazzo Pitti (entrance) and between the Forte di Belvedere and the Porta Romana (see entries) can be found the 111 acres (45 hectares) of the Boboli Gardens which owe their name to the Bogoli or Bogolini family. Work on this splendid park, perfect for long walks, was begun between 1550 and 1560 by Niccolò de' Pericoli (known as "Tribolo" – the

Location
Piazza Pitti

Buses
11, 36, 37

Giardino di Boboli

Opening times
Nov.–Feb.: 9 a.m.–4.30 p.m.;
Mar., Apr., Sept. and Oct.:
9 a.m.–5.30 p.m..;
May–Aug.: 9 a.m.–6.30 p.m.
Admission free

Fontana del Bacco

Grotta di Buontalenti

Amphitheatre

Neptune Fountain

Statue of Abundance

Giardino del Cavaliere

Museo delle Porcellane

Opening times
Tues.–Sat.
9 a.m.–2 p.m.
Sun. 9 a.m.–1 p.m.
Closed
Mon.

tormented), continued by Bernardo Buontalenti (1585–8) and completed by Alfonso Parigi the Younger (1628–58).
There are various interesting features in the gardens, considered to be one of the finest Mannerist sites of its kind:

NE of the Palazzo Pitti stands the Baccus Fountain, created in 1560. The figure riding on a tortoise represents the court dwarf of Cosimo I.

Near the fountain is the grotto created by Buontalenti (1533–1588) with statues of Ceres and Apollo, plaster casts of Michelangelo's "Slaves" and a Venus by Giambologna.

The amphitheatre, opposite the SE façade of the Palazzo Pitti, was built in 1618 by Giulio and Alfonso Parigi, and reconstructed in 1700. It was used by the Grand Dukes for their magnificent festivities. The obelisk comes from Egypt and the granite basin from Rome.

SE of the amphitheatre is the Neptune Fountain by Stoldo Lorenzi (1565). Neptune stands on a rock surrounded by Tritons and Sirens.

The colossal statue of "Dovizia" by Giambologna can be seen on the SE side of the park.

The "Garden of the Cavalier" is laid out on a terrace above the old city wall ramparts.
Silkworms were once bred and the first potatoes in Italy were grown here. A monkey fountain is a feature of the garden.

Since 1973 the Porcelain Museum has been housed in the 18th c. Casino del Cavaliere. It contains Italian, French and German porcelain and a collection from Vienna formerly in the possession of the Grand Dukes of Tuscany.

Viottolone
This is the name of an avenue leading from the Giardino del Cavaliere to the Piazzale dell'Isolotto. It is lined with cypresses, chestnut oaks and parasol pines.

Piazzale del Isolotto
In the centre of the oval square (laid out in 1618) is a pool with, in the centre, a copy of Giambologna's Fountain of Oceanus (original in the Museo Nazionale del Bargello, see Palazzo del Bargello).

The sculptures at the feet of Oceanus represent the rivers Nile, Ganges and Euphrates.

Loggia del Bigallo (Museo del Bigallo)   J5

Location
Piazza S. Giovanni

Buses
6, 11

This typical late-Gothic building near the Duomo and the Battistero (see entries) was commissioned by the Confraternity of Mercy (Compagnia della Misericordia) as a place to "display" lost or abandoned children for adoption. The marble loggia and the little palace of which it is part were built between 1353 and 1358 (probably by Ambrogio di Renzo). In 1445 Ventura di Moro and Rossello di Jacopo Franchi painted the walls under the double arches with frescoes of scenes from the life of St Peter, but the ones there now are only copies. Some of the originals are to be seen in the town hall inside the palace, which also houses works of 14th and 15th c. Florentine artists.

** Loggia dei Lanzi   J6

Also known as the Loggia della Signoria, the Loggia dei Lanzi owes its name to the guard of German lancers stationed here by Cosimo I.

Known, too, as the Loggia dell'Orcagna (after the famous artist Orcagna who may well have designed it), it was built between 1376 and 1382 under the direction of Benci di Cione and Simone di Francesco Talenti. The arcade, one of the finest examples of Florentine Gothic architecture, was used by the Republic for official ceremonies. This is where ambassadors and princes were received and where the Priors and the Gonfaloniere were formally proclaimed.

With the fall of the Republic the Loggia lost this political function and assumed a purely decorative role. After it was restored in the last century it resumed its original official use, and is now once again decked out with tapestries and garlands on festive occasions.

Above the round arches are panels with allegorical figures of the cardinal and theological virtues made by various artists to designs by Agnolo Gaddi (1384–9). On the roof is a terrace from which there is access to the Uffizi Gallery (see Palazzo e Galleria degli Uffizi).

Location
Piazza della Signoria

Buses
14, 19, 23, 31, 32

At present closed owing to structural weakness

Exterior

Loggia dei Lanzi: the arcade

Loggia di Mercato Nuovo

Museum

Inside the arcade is a small museum containing some important sculptures.

To the right and left of the entrance are two lions, one from Classical Greece and the other a 16th c. copy (Vacca).

On a clockwise tour of the museum the visitor's gaze immediately falls on the bronze statue of Perseus by Benvenuto Cellini (1545–54), an impressive masterpiece because of its delicacy of workmanship and bold composition.

In the centre of the wall diagonally opposite is the "Rape of Polyxena" in marble by Pio Ferdi (1866), followed by Classical statues of women along the back wall (very much restored). In the centre of the other side is another marble group, Giambologna's "Hercules fighting with Nessus the Centaur" (1599).

At the front is another masterpiece, "The Rape of the Sabines", a lively marble group of figures also by Giambologna (1583). It is said that the work was not given this title until later, so the artist was clearly chiefly making use of the theme of youthful manly strength, womanly beauty and old age to demonstrate his skill and his art.

*Loggia di Mercato Nuovo (Loggia of the New Market)   J6

Location
Via di Porta Rossa

Buses
B, 6, 11, 14, 19, 23, 31, 32

The Loggia di Mercato Nuovo, built by Del Tasso (1547–51) and formerly frequented by silk-merchants and goldsmiths, is today the market for Florentine handicrafts. The hall, which is open on all sides, is supported by 20 columns.

Fontana del Porcellino

Next to it is the "Fontana del Porcellino" or "Fountain of the Little Pig" as Pietro Tacca's bronze wild boar (1612) is popularly known. Tourist throw coins into the fountain and make a wish to return to Florence.

Loggia di San Paolo   H5

Location
Piazza Santa Maria Novella

Buses
9, 13, 14, 17, 19, 22, 23, 36, 37

Opposite the church of Santa Maria Novella (see entry), on the S side of the square, is the Loggia di San Paolo which was commissioned in 1466 by the head of the Ospedale di San Paolo. It is modelled closely on Brunelleschi's Loggia degli Innocenti (the Porch of the Foundling Hospital). The columns were replaced in 1789. It is decorated with terracotta medallions by the Florentine artists Andrea and Giovanni della Robbia.

Medici Chapel

See San Lorenzo, Cappelle Medicee

Michelangelo House and Museum

See Casa Buonarroti

Monumento di Carlo Goldoni (Carlo Goldoni Memorial) H6

The monument to the famous Italian dramatist Carlo Goldoni (1707–93), erected here by Ulisse Cambi in 1873, is the main feature of the square by the Arno, where seven streets converge, which bears the Venetian comedy playwright's name.

Location
Piazza Goldoni

Mosaic Museum

See Opificio e Museo delle Pietre Dure

Museo dell'Antica Casa Fiorentina (Museum of the Old Florentine House)

See Palazzo Davanzati

*Museo Archeologico Centrale dell'Etruria K5
(Archaeological Museum)

This is the most important archaeological museum in Northern Italy. Founded in 1870 its principal exhibits are finds from the areas of Italy settled by the Etruscans, as well as Egyptian, Greek and Roman antiquities. Collections begun by the Medici family are kept here. It is housed in the Palazzo della Crocetta which was built in 1620 for the Grand Duchess Maria Magdalena of Austria.

Location
Via della Colonna 36

Buses
1, 4, 6, 7, 10, 11, 17, 25, 34

Opening times
Tues.–Sat. 9 a.m.–2 p.m.,
Sun. and public holidays
9 a.m.–1 p.m.

Closed
Mon.

The museum is divided into the Topographical Museum of Etruria, the Egyptian Museum and the Museum of Etruscan, Greek and Roman Antiquities (Antiquarium Etrusco-Greco-Romano).

The Topographical Museum has a collection of finds from Etruria which provides a good illustration of the highly civilized and cultured life of the Etruscans (brightly colored sarcophagus of the Larthia Seianti (between 217 and 147 B.C., from Martinella near Chiusi). In the garden can be seen reconstructions of graves and funerary monuments.

Museo Topografico dell'
Etruria

The Egyptian Museum, which ranks second in importance to the one in Turin, has statues, busts, ceramics, reliefs, sarcophagi, mummies, pictures and utensils from various Egyptian dynasties, including a very well-preserved wooden chariot (from the time of Rameses I, 14th c. B.C.).

Egyptian Museum

The Etrusco-Greco-Romano department has displays of Etruscan urns and sarcophagi, including the Ramta Uzenai marble sarcophagus from Tarquinia; Etruscan, Greek and Roman bronzes, including the famous "Idolino" – the Greek statue of a young ephebe, a young man undergoing military training, (5th c. B.C.), the "Horse's Head" – a Greek bronze from the Roman period, the "Chimaera" – an Etruscan bronze with the body of a lion, the head of a ram and a serpent's tail, the "Orator" (dedicated to Aulus Metellus, 3rd c. B.C.) and a statue of Minerva, a copy of a Greek work found in Arezzo in 1554.

Antiquarium Etrusco-Greco-
Romano

Also of interest: the coin rooms with collections of coins minted in Etruria, medieval and modern Roman coins, and Italian coins; the collection of precious stones with gems, cameos and gold and silver articles, and the collection of vases with the famous "François Vase", painted by Klitias in the studio of the Greek Ergotimos (6th c. B.C.).

Other collections

SECONDO PIANO

PRIMO PIANO

Museo Archeologico

SECOND FLOOR (SECONDO PIANO)
   Museum of Etruscan, Greek and Roman Archaeology (continuation)
1, 2 Prehistoric department
3–6 Italian and Mediterranean comparisons
7–15 Vases of various origins, Etruscan terracottas and sculptures
16 Temporarily closed
17–30 Etruscan urns, sarcophagi, objects found in tombs, wall-paintings

FIRST FLOOR (PRIMO PIANO)
1–8 Museo Egiziano (Egyptian Museum): statues, reliefs, papyri, amulets, sarcophagi, mummies, a chariot made of Syrian wood
9–22 Museum of Etruscan, Greek and Roman Archaeology: Etruscan scuptures, sarcophagi, bronzes, coins, jewellery

Also worth seeing: the Etruscan Gallery of Plaster Casts, the Gallery of Etruscan Painting, the collection of hieroglyphics begun by Lorenzo de' Medici (the Magnificent) and the prehistoric department.

Museo degli Argenti (Silver Collection)

See Palazzo Pitti

Museo Bardini (Bardini Museum)   K7

Location
Piazza de' Mozzi 1

Buses
13n, 19, 23r, 31, 32, 33

Opening times
Mon., Tues., Thurs.–Sat.
9 a.m.–2 p.m., Sun. and
public holidays 8 a.m.–1 p.m.

Closed
Wed.

The Bardini Museum houses sculptures, paintings, furniture, ceramics, tapestries, arms, etc. from the Classical, Renaissance and Baroque periods. The collection was bequeathed to the city of Florence in 1923 by the art dealer Stefano Bardini. It is now on show to the public in the 19th c. palace where he lived.
Among the interesting works are a Caritas, an allegory of Love by Tino di Camaino and three by Donatello; also a small plaster "Deposition" by Michelangelo.
On the upper floor is the Galleria Corsa, an art collection bequeathed to Florence by Fortunata Carobbi in 1937. It consists of paintings in different styles and from various epochs.

Museo delle Carrozze (Coach Museum)

See Palazzo Pitti

Museo della Fondazione Horne (Horne Museum)   K6

The English art critic Herbert Percy Horne (1864–1916) gave the State a valuable collection of paintings, sculptures, drawings, furniture and ancient ornaments and utensils which are now on display in the Palazzetto Horne.
This building, also transferred to the State, was built in the late 15th c. for the Alberti family, probably by Simone del Pollaiolo ("Cronaca"), and later belonged to the Corsi family. The collection was seriously damaged in the 1966 floods (especially the exhibits on the ground floor. The rooms are currently being restored). The first floor houses 14th–16th c. paintings, including works by Simone Martini, Benozzo Gozzoli, Pietro Lorenzetti, Filippino Lippi and Bernardo Daddi.
Among the exhibits on the second floor are furniture made in Florence, drawings, roundels and terracottas (all 15th/16th c.).

Location
Via de' Benci 6

Buses
13r, 14, 19, 23, 31, 32

Opening times
Mon.–Sat. 9 a.m.–1 p.m.

Closed
Sun.

Museo Mediceo (Medici Museum)

See Palazzo Medici-Riccardi

Museo Nazionale di Antropologia ed Etnologia (Museum of Mankind)

See Palazzo Nonfinito

**Museo Nazionale del Bargello (National Museum)

See Palazzo del Bargello e Museo Nationale

Museo dell'Opera del Duomo (Cathedral Museum)   K5
(Museo di Santa Maria del Fiore)

A host of artists created notable works of art – sculpture, articles in gold and silver, embroidery, etc. – to furnish the Cathedral, the Campanile and the Baptistry (see entries). These could not be allowed to remain in their original positions because they were at risk from the weather and on security grounds so at an early stage they were removed for safekeeping. Since 1891 they have been kept in the Cathedral Museum, which from the 15th c. had also served as studios and workshops for the artists and craftsmen working on the cathedral.

Some of the most interesting exhibits are mentioned below.

Entrance
Above the portal of the Museo dell'Opera del Duomo (named after the cathedral building works) is a bust of Grand Duke Cosimo I (1572, by Giovanni Bandini).

Anteroom
Among the items in the anteroom is a bust of Brunelleschi, the creator of the dome of the cathedral.

Location
Piazza del Duomo 9

Buses
1, 6, 7, 10, 11, 13r, 14, 17, 19r, 22, 23, 25, 32, 33

Opening times
Mon.–Sat. 9 a.m.–6 p.m.; (in summer until 8 p.m.) Sun. 10 a.m.–1 p.m.

Ground floor

Donatello's cantoria

"Room of the old façade of the cathedral"
This room contains statues that were incorporated in the old façade of the cathedral and which were removed before it was demolished in 1587. There is also a drawing dating from the second half of the 16th c. showing the old façade of the Duomo (on the right of the entrance).

Among the most interesting works are: along the wall left of the entrance the statue of St Luke (by Nanni di Banco), the statue of John the Evangelist (by Donatello) and the statue of St Matthew (by Bernardo Ciuffagni); along the left-hand wall the statue of Pope Boniface VIII (by Arnolfo di Cambio). On the wall opposite the entrance the statue of "S. Reparata", the statue of the "Madonna and Child" and the statue of the "Madonna of the Nativity" (all by Arnolfo di Cambio).

On the right-hand wall the statue "The Virgin interred in the Sepulchre" (plaster cast; by Arnolfo di Cambio) and the statues of St Augustine and St Gregory (by Niccolò di Piero Lamberti).

Small room

In the "Small Room" are missals (damaged by the 1966 floods), precious reliquaries and other items of gold and silver from the cathedral treasury.

Also of interest is the original wooden model for the lantern of the cathedral with Brunelleschi's signature in his own hand.

Goldsmiths' octagon
This contains relics from the period 1300–1800.

Mezzanine
First floor

On the mezzanine is Michelangelo's "Pietà".

Sala delle Cantorie
The "Room of the Cantoria" contains the two marble choir-gallery parapets or cantoria which used to support the console

of the cathedral organ. Until 1686 they stood below the dome and were dismantled on the occasion of the wedding of Grand Duke Cosimo III and Violante Beatrice of Bavaria.

To the left of the entrance is the Cantoria by Luca della Robbia (1431–8), while opposite is the Cantoria by Donatello. The famous wooden figure of "Mary Magdalene" by Donatello, which was brought here from the Battistero (see entry) is under Donatello's choral gallery.

Against the left-hand wall are the statues of John the Baptist (1423–7) and Habakkuk, popularly known as "Lo Zuccone", i.e. Baldhead (1434–6), both by Donatello.

To the right of the entrance is Donatello's sculpture of Abraham and Isaac (1421).

Sala delle Formelle del Campanile di Giotto

This room contains the bas-reliefs which formerly decorated the panels on the lower storey of Giotto's Campanile (see Duomo Santa Maria del Fiore, Campanile); these were replaced by copies between 1965 and 1967. The panels with the allegorical figures are by Andrea Pisano (first two bottom panels on the long right-hand wall, bottom row on right-hand wall opposite, bottom row on the long left-hand wall, bottom row on left-hand wall opposite), Luca della Robbia (bottom row on the long right-hand wall), by artists of the school of Pisano (top row on the right-hand wall opposite, top row on the long left-hand wall, top row on the left-hand wall opposite) and Alberto Arnoldi (top row, long right-hand wall).

Sala dell'Altare

The greatest treasures of the Altar Room are the silk and gold needlework panels with scenes from the life of St John the Baptist, from designs by Antonio Pollaiolo (long left-hand wall) and the silver altar of the Battistero (left-hand wall opposite), one of the finest examples of the art of the Florentine silversmiths. It was begun in the Gothic style in 1366 and completed during the Renaissance (1480). The altar is decorated with prophets and sibyls, scenes from the life of John the Baptist and other scenes from the scriptures.

The other works in the room are by 14th and 15th c. artists (including Giovanni della Robbia, Tino da Camaino, Giovanni di Balduccio, Giovanni Bandini and Andrea Pisano).

Michelangelo's Pietà

Since 1981 one of the most famous sculptures of Western art has been kept in the cathedral museum – Michelangelo's Pietà, the marble group created by the artist in his old age but never completed. The limp, broken figure of the lifeless Christ, the face of Mary with only a hint of her suffering, the grief-stricken visage of Nicodemus, possibly a self-portrait, the unfulfilled nature of the whole group (the figure of Mary Magdalene on the left was added later) – all this combines in an incomparable expression of the concept of death and man's helplessness in the face of mortality. Michelangelo smashed this statue because he was not satisfied with his own work. His pupil Calcagni reassembled the fragments and, except for the figure of Christ, added the finishing touches.

Museo dell'Opera di Santa Croce

See Santa Croce

Museo Stibbert: housed in the Villa Montughi

Museo di San Marco

See San Marco

Museo Stibbert (Stibbert Museum)

Location
Via Frederico Stibbert 26

Bus
1

Opening times
Mon.–Wed., Fri., Sat. 9 a.m.–
2 p.m.; Sun. and public
holidays 9 a.m.–12.30 p.m.

From 1860 onwards the Scottish officer Frederick Stibbert collected art treasures in the Villa Montughi just outside the city. In 1906 he gave them to the city of Florence.

The collection of arms is especially interesting; in the huge "Cavalcade Room" is a row of horsemen with uniforms and weapons from various countries, and further exhibits – furniture, paintings, textiles and other works of artistic value – show the feeling for art and the taste of the collector.

Museo Storico Topografico – Firenze com'era   K5
(Historical Museum – Florence as it used to be)

Location
Via dell'Oriuolo 4 (opposite
Santa Maria Nuova)

Buses
4, 9, 14, 17, 19, 22, 23, 36,
37

In the old convent of the Oblates with its fine 15th c. cloister can be found a collection of paintings, drawings, prints and photographs that show how the city of Florence has developed since the end of the 15th c.
It also shows the everyday life of the people of Florence, their various festivals and their great processions.
Open on weekdays (except Thursdays) from 9 a.m. to 2 p.m. and on Sundays and public holidays from 8 a.m.to 1 p.m.

Museo Zoologico "La Specola" (Zoological Museum)   H7

The Zoological Museum is in the Palazzo Torrigiani, also known as "La Specola" i.e. "the observatory", because Grand Duke Pietro Leopoldo built an astronomical and meteorological observatory here in 1775.
The museum's collection of anatomical specimens in wax is particularly interesting.
The museum is open on Tuesdays and Thursdays from 9 a.m. to noon and on Sundays from 9.30 a.m. to 12.30 p.m. The department of anatomy is open during the summer (except in the second half of August and the whole of September) from 3 to 6 p.m. Admission is free.

Location
Via Romana 17

Bus
B

Museum of the History of Science

See Palazzo Castellanti

* Ognissanti (All Saints' Church)   H5

The church of "Ognissanti" (All Saints), one of the first Baroque churches in Florence, dates back to a 13th c. building but was completely renovated in the 16th and 17th c. Restoration work had to be carried out in 1872 and after the severe flooding in 1966.
The main features of the exterior are the terracotta "Coronation of the Virgin with Saints", ascribed to both Giovanni della Robbia and Benedetto Buglioni, and the Romanesque Campanile.

Of interest in the interior:
At the second altar on the right there is Domenico Ghirlandaio's "Madonna della Misericordia" ("Madonna of the Protecting Cloak", 1470) and a fresco with a Pietà by Domenico and Davide Ghirlandaio (1472).

Sacristy
The sacristy contains a painting on wood of "Christ Crucified" in the style of Giotto and a fresco of the Crucifixion by Taddeo Gaddi.

Cloister of the old monastery
Entered through the transept or from the square. It consists of Ionic columns. The frescoes with scenes from the "Life of St Francis" (17th c.) are currently being restored.

Refectory
Famous frescoes are also to be found in the refectory: Domenico Ghirlandaio's "Last Supper" and "St Jerome in his Study" (1480) as well as Sandro Botticelli's famous "Saint Augustine in his Chamber".

Location
Piazza Ognissanti

Buses
6, 9, 11, 36

Opificio e Museo delle Pietre Dure   K5
(Mosaic Workshops and Museum)

The so-called "Florentine mosaic", semi-precious stones inlaid in stone, has a long and unique tradition. Skilled craftsmen

Location
Via degli Alfani 78

Orsanmichele

Buses
B, 4, 11, 17

Opening times
9 a.m.–2 p.m.

Closed
Public Holidays

were especially in demand for the princes' chapel of San Lorenzo (see entry) in 1588. They started up in shops in the Palazzo degli Uffizi (see entry) and then after 1796 moved to the Convent of San Niccolò where this special Florentine craft is still carried on today.

Also to be found here is a museum full of interesting examples of the art of these consummate craftsmen.

Orsanmichele (San Michele in Orto; Church)   J6

Location
Via Arte della Lana 1

Buses
B, 6, 11, 14, 19, 23, 31, 32

Opening times
7 a.m.–noon, 2–7 p.m. daily

The present church, a very well-preserved 14th c. building, developed from an oratory (Orsanmichele is the abbreviated form of San Michele in Orto) and granary. These housed a miraculous picture that came to attract more worshippers than buyers. As a result the building's religious function was given precedence at the end of the 14th c.

The delicate articulation of the external walls, its ornamentation, arches, niches, figures, mouldings, the marble infill in the window openings and the uncluttered tracery of the pillared arcades raise the church high in the architectural rankings.

The beauty of the architecture is complemented by important works of sculpture.

Exterior

The painstakingly and artistically wrought niches (or tabernacles) on the façade, commissioned by the individual guilds in the city, contain the guilds' patron saints.

On the Via dei Calzaiuoli side:
Left Lorenzo Ghiberti's "St John the Baptist" (1414), the first major Renaissance bronze statue; in the next niche (by Donatello) "Incredulity of St Thomas", a major work by Andrea del Verrocchio (c. 1480); right "St Luke" by Giambologna (1600).

On the Via dei Lamberti (S) side
"St Mark", an early work by Donatello (1411); "St James" by Lamberti (c. 1422); "Madonna delle Rose" (1399, probably by Piero di Giovanni Tedesco) and "St John the Evangelist" by Baccio da Montelupo (1515).

W façade
"St Matthew", Lorenzo Ghiberti's most important large statue (1419–22), "St Stephen", also by Ghiberti (1428), and Nanni di Banco's "St Eligius" (1415).

N side
"St Peter" (1408–13) attributed to Donatello. "St Philip" (1415) and "Four Crowned Saints" (1408), a group of four martyrs, both works by Nanni di Banco, and Donatello's "St George" (1418; copy, original in the Museo Nazionale del Bargello, see Palazzo del Bargello).

Interior

The interior of the two-naved church is impressive on account of its frescoes, paintings and stained-glass windows.

In the left-hand nave is the altar of St Anne with Francesco da Sangallo's marble sculpture "Madonna and Child with St Anne" (1526).

At the back of the right-hand nave is Orcagna's famous Gothic marble tabernacle (1349–59), the rich ornamentation of which sets off the miraculous picture of the Madonna (by Bernardo Daddi, 1347). Reliefs on the plinth show scenes from the life of the Virgin (front) and "Death and Assumption of the Virgin" with a self-portrait of Orcagna (back, 1359).

The tabernacle is decorated with angels and prophets, sibyls, apostles and allegorical figures of the virtues. Pietro Migliore's marble grille with a bronze trellis (1366) is also an interesting feature.

Opposite Orsanmichele is the small but interesting church of San Carlo dei Lombardi (see entry).

Orti Oricellari (Oricellari Gardens)   H5

Adjacent to the Palazzo Venturi-Ginori is part of the famous Orti Oricellari. To this garden Bernardo Rucellai transferred the Accademia Platonica (Philosophers' Academy) in 1498. The Academy was visited by Pope Leo X (1516) and Emperor Charles V (1530).
In the centre of the garden is a colossal statue of Polyphemus (27·6 ft – 8·4 m high) by Antonio Novelli, a pupil of Giambologna.

Location
Via degli Orti Oricellari

Buses
A, 4, 9, 13, 14, 17, 22, 23, 26, 27, 28, 29, 30, 35

Orto Botanico (Botanical garden; officially: Giardino dei Semplici)   K4/5

The "Giardino dei Semplici" was founded in 1545 by Cosimo I for the study of exotic plants. It is the headquarters of the Italian Botanical Society, the "Società Botanica Italiana", and together with the school and the museum forms part of the "Institute of Botany".
The garden and the museum are open on Mondays, Wednesdays and Fridays from 9 a.m. until midday, admission is free.

Location
Via la Pira 4

Buses
4, 6, 7, 10, 11, 17, 20

Museo Botanico

Palazzo Altoviti-Valori   K6

The Palazzo Altoviti in Borgo degli Albizi, a street with many fine town houses, first belonged to the Albizi family and then to the Valori and Guicciardini families.
In the 16th c. Baccio Valori decorated it with busts of famous Florentines (Ficino, Vespucci, Alberti, Guicciardini, Dante, Petrarch, Boccaccio and others) which is why it became disrespectfully known by the locals as "the Rogues' Gallery".

Location
Borgo degli Albizi 18

Buses
13, 14, 19, 23, 31, 32

Palazzo Antinori   J5

In Piazza Antinori, opposite the church of San Gaetano, is the town house of the Antinori family. The severe and elegant palace was built between 1461 and 1466 in the style of Giuliano da Maiano.
For many generations the Antinoris have devoted themselves to the production of good wine. (There is a wine bar in the palace.)

Location
Piazza Antinori 3

Buses
A, 1, 6, 7, 10, 22, 25

Palazzo Arcivescovile (Archbishop's Palace) J5

Location
Piazza San Giovanni

Buses
1, 6, 7, 10, 11, 13, 14, 17, 19, 23, 25, 31, 32, 33

The Archbishop's Palace was built between 1573 and 1584 by Giovanni Antonio Dosio for Cardinal Alessandro Medici who later became Pope Leo XI, but it was not finally completed until 1735, by Ciurini. During this long period it developed into a mixture of medieval and "modern" elements. In 1895 the whole palace was moved back 50 yards to make room for the city's growing traffic.

Palazzo dell'Arte della Lana J6

Location
Via dell'Arte della Lana

Buses
B, 6, 11

Florence prospered in the Middle Ages by producing and processing wool and selling the finished products. This is evident in the palace of the guild of weavers and wool merchants which had 200 shops and employed 30,000 workmen. The irregular palace complex, linked to the church of Orsanmichele (see entry) by a bridge (built in 1569 by Buontalenti), was begun in 1308. After it was restored in 1905 it became the headquarters of the Dante Society. Today the palace houses a shop, and cross vaults can be seen in its showrooms.

A bridge gives access to the interior rooms, the Saloni di Orsanmichele, which contain fine paintings (Taddeo Gaddi's "Entombment"). On the corner of Via dell'Arte della Lana and Via Orsanmichele is the 14th c. Gothic tabernacle of Santa Maria della Tromba.

** Palazzo del Bargello e Museo Nazionale K6
(Bargello Palace and National Museum)

Location
Via del Proconsolo 4

Buses
13, 14, 19, 23, 31, 32

Opening times
Tues. –Sat 9 a.m.–2 p.m.,
Sun. and public holidays
9 a.m.–1 p.m.

Closed
Mon.

The huge bulk of the sturdy tower and crenellated walls of the Bargello, the massive palace which the citizens of Florence built after 1250 as testimony to their victory over the nobility, is one of the city's landmarks. Located in Piazza San Firenze, between Via del Proconsolo, Via della Vigna Vecchia, Via dell'Acqua and Via Ghibellina, nowadays it houses the National Museum (photo on p. 65).

In 1261 it became the seat of the Podestà, the governing body of the city. After 1502 this was the site of the Rota (ecclesiastical court) and prison and in 1574 the palace became the seat of the Bargello (chief constable). In 1859 Italy's first national museum and most important collection of sculpture (apart from those in the Vatican) was installed in the palace.

**Museo Nazionale del Bargello (National Museum)

Opening times
Tues.–Sat. 9 a.m.–2 p.m.;
Sun. and public holidays
9 a.m.–1 p.m.

The National Museum contains works by important 14th–16th c. Tuscan sculptors (especially Donatello, della Robbia and Michelangelo). Closed Mon.

Ground floor

Courtyard
The courtyard is worth visiting for its architecture alone. It is surrounded on three sides by an arcade (round arches,

octagonal columns, groin vaulting). On the fourth side an open staircase leads to the upper floors.

Pillars and walls are decorated with the coats of arms of the Podestà, the members of the Rota and the quarters and boroughs of the city. In the centre of the courtyard is an octagonal pillar. Nearby is where the scaffold used to stand when the Bargello was also a prison.

Today the courtyard and arcade are used to display sculpture. There are works on view by Niccolò di Piero Lamberti, Vincenzo Danti, Cosimo Cenni, Vincenzo Gemito, Bartolomeo Ammannati, Domenico Poggini and Giambologna.

Michelangelo Room

The courtyard leads into the rooms containing works by Michelangelo: "Brutus", a marble statue (c. 1540); "Madonna and Child with the young John the Baptist", a circular relief, carved for Bartolomeo Pitti about 1504; "David" (c. 1531), also known as "Little Apollo"; "Drunken Bacchus", Michelangelo's first large sculpture (1497–9).

Other works are by 16th c. artists. Worthy of particular mention are Jacopo Sansovino's statue of Bacchus (c. 1520), the bronze bust of Michelangelo by Daniele da Volterra, the bust of Cosino I by Benvenuto Cellini (1557) and other of Cellini's works, including his marble statue of Narcissus (1540).

First Floor

Loggia

The Loggia on the first floor has Giambologna's bronze statue of Mercury (1564), his important allegory of "Architecture", and sculptures by Baccio Bandinelli and Francesco Moschino.

Grand Hall

This contains statues by Donatello, including his "St George" (1416, marble statue formerly in a niche in the church of Orsanmichele), "Marble David" (1408–9), "Bronze David" (made in 1430 for Cosimo the Elder), "St John as a Child" (Casa Martelli) and the "Marzocco Lion" (1420). Other artists represented in this room are Desiderio da Settignano, Vecchietta, Luca della Robbia and Bertoldo di Giovanni. Filippo Brunelleschi's and Lorenzo Ghiberti's models for the competition for the N portal of the Battistero (see entry) complete the display.

Also on display on the first floor are frescoes in the Chapel of the Podestà, ivory carvings (Ivory Room), a collection of majolica (Majolica Room) and the work of enamellers and goldsmiths (Room of the Goldsmiths).

Second floor

Verrocchio Room

As its name implies, this room chiefly contains works by Verrocchio, including his "Noblewoman", "David" (bronze), "Madonna and Child" (high relief) and "Resurrection of Christ" (high relief).

Other artists represented in this room are Antonio Rossellino, Mino da Fiesole, Antonio del Pollaiolo, Francesco Laurana and Matteo Civitati.

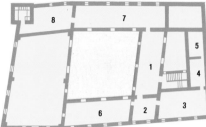

SECONDO PIANO

Palazzo del Bargello

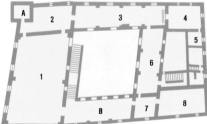

PRIMO PIANO

Museo Nazionale

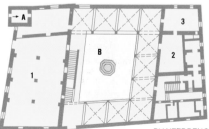

PIANTERRENO

SECOND FLOOR (SECONDO PIANO)
1. Sala di G. della Robbia
   Glazed terracottas, by Della Robbia, plus works by Rustici, Bandinelli, Giambologna
2. Sala di A. della Robbia
3. Sala del Verrocchio
   Busts and reliefs, by Verrocchio and others
4, 5 Medici collection of coins and medals
6. Sala del Camino
   Small bronze figures
7. Sala delle Armi
   Collection of weapons
8. Sala della Torre
   Tapestries, textiles

FIRST FLOOR (PRIMO PIANO)
A Tower
B Loggia
   "Mercury" and "Allegory of Architecture", by Giambologna. Works by 15th and 16th c. Florentine artists
1. Salone del Consiglio Generale or Salone di Donatello
   "San Giorgio", "San Giovannino", "David", "Il Marzocco", by Donatello, "Il Sacrificio di Isacco", by Brunelleschi. Works by L. della Robbia, Ghiberti, Michelozzo
2. Sala della Torre
   Tapestries, etc. from Germany and Asia Minor (15th and 16th c.)
3. Salone del Podestà
   Enamels and goldsmiths' work
4. Cappella del Podestà
   Frescoes, probably by Giotto
5. Sagrestia
   Frescoes (14th c.)
6. Sala degli Avori
   Wood carvings (14th and 16th c.), ivory carvings
7. Sala delle Oreficerie
   Jewelry, coins, enamels, silver goblets
8. Sala delle Maioliche
   Majolica (15th and 16th c.)

GROUND FLOOR (PIANTERRENO)
A Entrance and vestibule
B Courtyard with octagonal fountain
1. Michelangelo Room
   "David" (c 1531), "Brutus" (1540), "Drunken Bacchus" (c. 1498), by Michelangelo "Bacchus", by Sansovino Bust of Cosimo I, by Cellini Costanza Bonarelli, by Bernini
2. Gothic sculpture room
3. 14th c. Florentine sculpture, inc. works by T. di Camaino, A. Arnoldi, S. Talenti, Arnolfo di Cambio

Palazzo Bartolini Salimbeni

Great Hall: statues by Donatello

Andrea Robbia Room
Glazed terracottas by this artist.

Giovanni della Robbia Room
Glazed terracottas by Giovanni della Robbia.

Coin collection
Two rooms contain the famous Medici coin collection that was
started by Lorenzo de' Medici and constantly added to by his
successors.

Also on display on the second floor are tapestries and textiles
from Florence (Tower Room), 13th–17th c. weapons (Armoury)
and a collection of small bronze figures (Fireplace Room).

Palazzo Bartolini Salimbeni J6

Location
Piazza S. Trinità

Buses
A, 6, 11

This palace was built between 1517 and 1520 by Baccio
d'Agnolo and thoroughly restored in 1962. The people of
Florence reproached the architect with having used too many
Roman elements (the Classical forms of Bramante and
Raphael) more suited to a church than to a town house. The
architect responded by inscribing above the portal "carpere
promptius quam imitari" ("it is easier to carp than to imitate").
Another inscription above the windows gives the clue to the
secret of the success of the former occupants: "Per non
dormire" ("By not sleeping").

Palazzo dei Capitani di Parte Guelfa (Or Palazzo di Parte Guelfa) J6

The palace's Gothic windows, the covered open staircase and
the merlons hark back to the 14th c. In the power struggle
between the Guelphs and the Ghibellines, i.e. the supporters of
the Pope and of the Holy Roman Emperor, that engulfed the
towns and cities of Italy in the 13th c., this house is where the
Capitani di Parte Guelfa held in trust the property confiscated
from the defeated Ghibellines.
The 15th c. alterations were directed by the architects
Brunelleschi and Francesco della Luna.
The medieval palace contains splendid rooms with harmonious proportions. The ceilings and walls were decorated by
Giambologna, Luca della Robbia, Donatello and others.
Today the palace houses the head offices of various
organisations.

Location
Piazza de Parte Guelfa

Bus
B

Palazzo Castellani con Museo di Storia della Scienza J6
(Museum of the History of Science)

From 1574 to 1841 this severe medieval building that looks like
a fort was the headquarters of the Rota court (hence the name
of the square, "Giudici"=judges). Since 1930 the palace has
housed the Museum of the History of the Experimental
Sciences. It was seriously damaged in the 1966 floods.
In the collection are instruments and scientific objects, some
belonging to the Medici and some from other Florentine
institutes: optical and mathematical apparatus, including a
mechanical writing device, electrical apparatus, instruments
for astronomy and cosmography and physical and anatomical
models.
One room is devoted to Galileo and his discoveries.

Location
Piazza dei Giudici 1

Buses
13n, 19n, 31, 32, 33

Opening times
Mon.–Sat. 9.30 a.m.–1 p.m.;
Mon., Wed., Fri. 2–5 p.m.

Closed
Sun., public holidays

Palazzo Corsini con Galleria Corsini (Art Gallery) H6

The Palazzo Corsini stands beside the Arno, and its impressive
façade is best viewed from the opposite bank (it is incomplete;
the left-hand wing that should offset the right-hand wing is
missing).
The palace, still owned by the Corsini family, was built by Pier
Francesco Silvani and Antonio Ferri (1648–56) in the 16th c.
style but also with occasional Baroque elements. The spiral
staircase inside the palace is one of the most important
examples of Baroque architecture in Florence.
The palace houses the most important private collection in
Florence (on the first floor), founded in 1765 by Lorenzo Corsini,
a nephew of Pope Clement XII. Unlike other museums the
pictures are not arranged chronologically but in accordance
with the old criterion of decoration and symmetry. A painting
should be part of the decoration of the room and not be looked
at for its own sake.
On display are fine examples of the Italian and foreign schools
of the 17th c. and of 15th and 16th c. Florentine painting
(including Raphael).
There are several statues and busts of Pope Clement XII
(1730–40) who was a member of the Corsini family.
The gallery can only be visited by prior arrangement;
tel. 21 89 94.

Location
Lungarno Corsini 10
(entrance Via di Parione 11)

Buses
A, 6, 11, 36, 37

Palazzo Davanzati con Museo dell'Antica Casa Fiorentina

Palazzo Corsini: view from the opposite bank of the Arno

*Palazzo Davanzati con Museo dell'Antica Casa Fiorentina   J6
(Museum of the Old Florentine House)

Location
Via Porta Rossa 13,
Piazza Davanzati

Buses
B, 6, 11, 36, 37

The severe five-storey façade of the Palazzo Davanzati is divided up on the ground floor by three massive doors, topped by a loggia and decorated in the centre by a splendid coat of arms of the Davanzati family (in summer the curtains are fastened to the iron bars in front of the windows).

The Davizzi built a town house here in 1300; one of the family was Gonfaloniere of the Republic in 1294. In the 16th c. the palace was acquired by the Bartolini family and later (1578) by the Davanzati. In 1906 the building was bought by the art dealer Elia Volpi and restored to its former glory. Since 1956 it has contained the "Museum of the Old Florentine House".

Museo dell'Antica Casa Fiorentina

Opening times
Tues.–Sat., 9 a.m.–2 p.m.;
Sun. 9 a.m.–1 p.m.

Closed
Mon.

The "Museum of the Old Florentine House" covers three floors and contains furniture, drawings, sculptures, tapestries, ceramics, textiles and everyday objects from the Middle Ages, the Renaissance and the Baroque period.

The "Parrot Room" on the first floor is especially interesting. It gets its name from its decoration. The walls are painted to look like tapestries with parrots. The room has a painted wooden ceiling.

The exhibits have been assembled from the Museo Nazionale del Bargello (see Palazzo del Bargello), other collections in Florence and from gifts. They provide a glimpse of the highly-cultivated life of the citizens of Florence who furnished their houses with valuable art treasures and utensils.

Palazzo Medici-Riccardi: built for Cosimo the Elder ▶

Palazzo Frescobaldi H/J6

Location
Piazza Frescobaldi 1

Buses
A, B

In the Piazza Frescobaldi, on the left bank of the Arno at the end of the Ponte Santa Trinità (see entry), stands the palace of the Frescobaldi family. Built in the 13th c., it was used by Charles de Valois, the brother of the French king, as his residence when his peace mission on behalf of Pope Boniface VIII brought him to Florence in 1301 (one of the consequences of his meditation was Dante's being sent into exile).
Next to it is the Baroque Palazzo dei Padri delle Missioni, today an Istituto Magistrale.

*Palazzo Gondi K6

Location
Piazza San Firenze 1

Buses
B, 19n, 23, 31, 32, 33

The Palazzo Gondi, one of the finest examples of 15th c. Florentine palaces, was built between 1490 and 1501 by Giuliano da Sangallo but not completed until 1874 by Poggi. The main feature of its façade is the way the stone has been meticulously worked on the individual stories becoming flatter towards the top.
The courtyard, one of the most charming of the Renaissance, is especially worth seeing. Here again one is struck by the careful use of the material and the artistic craftsmanship (on the capitals, the staircase and the fountain).

Palazzo Grifoni

See Palazzo Riccardi-Manelli

Palazzo Guadagni H6/7

Location
Piazza di Santo Spirito 10

Bus
B

The Palazzo in Piazza di Santo Spirito has a classical severity and beauty. Simone del Pollaiolo, known as Cronaca, built it (probably 1503–6) for Riniero Dei. The three stories in different styles, are topped by an open loggia.
In 1684 it was acquired by the Marchese Guadagni and later by the Dufour-Berte family.

**Palazzo Medici-Riccardi e Museo Mediceo (Medici Museum) J5

Location
Via Cavour 1 (Via Larga)/Via Gori

Buses
1, 4, 6, 7, 10, 11, 17, 25

The majestic bulk of the Palazzo Medici, opposite the church of San Lorenzo (see entry), bespeaks the power of a ruling dynasty. At the same time its limitation to the bare essentials testifies to the wise lack of ostentation of the Medici family at that time. They presided over a democratic-republican community and would never have chosen to behave like monarchs of the city.
The palace was built between 1444 and 1464 by Michelozzo for Cosimo the Elder. All the Medici princes lived and ruled here

until Cosimo I (1540) moved into the Palazzo Vecchio (see entry). In 1655 it was acquired by the Riccardi family who enlarged it by extending the side of the palace; in 1818 it was bought by the Grand Dukes of Tuscany. Today it houses the Medici Museum (ground floor) and the Prefecture (first floor). Its valuable art treasures and furnishings have been severely depleted through being plundered, destroyed or sold off.

An interesting feature of the façade is that each of the three stories are very different from the others. The windows on the ground floor are supported on brackets and therefore seem to be "kneeling". they are surmounted by wide arches and every other one has a triangular gable. The windows on the first floor have beautiful decoration, while the second floor is dominated by a heavy cornice.
On the corner opposite San Lorenzo (see entry) is the Medici coat of arms (six balls, the top one decorated with a lily).

Exterior

The interior of the palace was altered by the Riccardi family, and there are only a few of the original Medici rooms – on the ground floor, where the Medici Museum is, and on the first floor.
The archway leads into the square courtyard, with twelve marble medallions above the colonnade and the statue of Orpheus by Baccio Bandinelli, then comes the smaller garden courtyard.
The entrance to the Medici Museum, which opened in 1929, is in the main courtyard. The most interesting room on the first floor is the chapel, built by Michelozzo and covered in frescoes. The wall frescoes – "The Procession of the Magi to Bethlehem" – constitute one of the principal works of Benozzo Gozzoli.
Gozzoli incorporated two historical events into his cycle of frescoes: the magnificent assembly of bishops which took place in Florence in 1439 and which led to the union of the Roman and Greek churches, and the visit of Pope Pius II, the great humanist Aeneas Silvius Piccolomini, to Florence in 1459. There are portraits of some of the people who took part in these events including Joseph, the Patriarch of Constantinople (as the oldest of the Magi), John VI, Emperor in the East, and Lorenzo de' Medici (as a young boy).
The frescoes are very well preserved and with their bright colors present a vivid and lively picture of Florence in the 15th c. and the culture and prosperity of the Renaissance.
The altarpiece is a copy of Filippo Lippi's famous "Nativity".
In the Galleria di Luca Giordano is the "Apotheosis of the Second Medici Dynasty", an important fresco by Luca Giordano (1682–3).
The Galleria leads to the Biblioteca Riccardiana e Moreniana. It is worth having a look at the exhibition room: the vaulted ceiling is painted with frescoes by Luca Giordano (1683) on the allegorical theme of Intellect aiding Man to free himself from Enslavement by Stupidity.

Interior

Museo Mediceo (Medici Museum)

The Medici Museum, containing the works of art and furnishings acquired or owned by the Medici, keeps alive the memory of the great dynasty that made Florence one of the most famed cities of art in the West. A brief mention of some of

Opening times
Mon., Tues., Thurs.–Sat.
9 a.m.–12.30 p.m. 3–5 p.m.;
Sun. and public holidays
9 a.m.–noon

Closed
Wed.

the main exhibits is given below, with a recommendation to look at the unsullied architecture and tasteful décor of the rooms themselves.

Of especial interest: "Madonna and Child", one of Filippo Lippi's most important works (1442), the death-mask of Lorenzo the Magnificent, and a painting by Jacopo da Empolo, "The Wedding of Catherine de' Medici and Henri II of France" (1533).

Palazzo Nonfinito   K6

(Museo Nazionale di Antropologia ed Etnologia; Museum of Mankind)

Location
Via del Proconsolo 12

Buses
14, 19n, 23, 31, 32, 33

Opening times
1st and 3rd Sun. in month
9 a.m.–1 p.m.

Admission free

The Palazzo Nonfinito is, as its name suggests, unfinished, a fact belied by its exterior. Allessandro Strozzi commissioned the architect Bernardo Buontalenti to build a new town house for his family near the Palazzo Pazzi (see entry). Neither Buontalenti nor his successors, however, were able to complete the large building with the beautiful inner courtyard. Since 1869 the Palazzo has housed the Museo Nazionale di Antropologia ed Etnologia (Museum of Mankind) with anthropological and ethnological collections from all over the world.

Palazzo Pandolfini   K4

Location
Via San Gallo 74

Buses
B, 20, 34

The famous painter Raphael designed a palace for Giannozzo Pandolfini, the Bishop of Troia, and Giovanni Francesco and Aristotile da Sangallo put his plans into effect about 1520.

The charm of the palace lies in its simple elegance and the perfect expression of elements of the Roman Renaissance. It was originally intended to extend the palace to the right so that the portal would have been in the middle. However under Pope Clement VII, a Medici – his name can be seen next to that of Leo X on the right-hand side – it was obviously decided to leave the building half-finished.

Palazzo dei Pazzi   K6

Location
Via del Proconsolo 10,
Borgo degli Albizi

Buses
13r, 14, 19n, 23, 31, 32, 33

The palace was built for Jacopo de' Pazzi who was executed in 1478 after the conspiracy against Lorenzo and Giuliano de' Medici. The work was originally under the direction of Brunelleschi (1430) but was later taken over by Giuliano da Maiano (1462–72) whose contribution is marked by its meticulous execution and love for architectural detail.

The Pazzi family, who moved to Florence from Fiesole (see entry) in the Middle Ages, personified commercial acumen and hunger for power. Once Lorenzo de' Medici had survived their murder bid their attempt to break the power of the Medicis was doomed to failure. The family was banned and their palace was handed over to the Cibo family and later belonged to the Strozzis and Quarantesis.

Palazzo Pitti and Museums ·· H/J6/7

The Palazzo Pitti ranks as Florence's most important palace together with the Palazzo Vecchio (they are joined together by a passage) and the Palazzo Medici-Riccardi (see entries). Its size is impressive – it covers a surface area of 344,320 sq. ft (32,000 sq. m) and its façade is 224 yd (205 m) across and 118 ft (36 m) high at the center – and so is its architecture, an effect that is heightened by the way the square fronting it slopes slightly uphill towards it.

The art gallery (Galleria Palatina or Pitti) in the Palazzo Pitti is one of the most important in the world, almost on equal terms, so far as works of art are concerned, with the collections of the Uffizi (see Palazzo e Galleria degli Uffizi). The palace also houses the Museo degli Argenti (Silver Museum), the Galleria d'Arte Moderna (Gallery of Modern Art), the Contini Bonacassi collection, the Museo delle Carrozze (Carriage Museum) and the Appartamenti ex Reali (Royal Apartments).

In the adjoining Palazzina della Meridiana are the Galleria del Costume and the Collezione Contini Bonacossi (see Practical Information Section; Museums).

Location
Piazza Pitti

Bus
B

Opening times
Tues.–Sat. 9 a.m.–2 p.m.;
Sun. and public holidays
9 a.m.–1 p.m.

Closed
Mon.

Palazzo Pitti

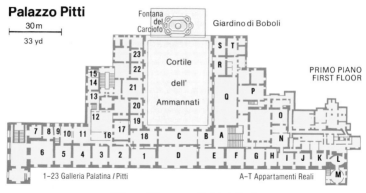

1–23 Galleria Palatina / Pitti   A–T Appartamenti Reali

1 Sala di Venere
  Titian, Tintoretto
2 Sala di Apollo
  Van Dyck, Rubens,
  Reni, del Sarto,
  Titian, Tintoretto
3 Sala di Marte
  Tintoretto, Reni,
  Titian, Rubens,
  Murillo, Veronese
4 Sala di Giove
  Raphael, Bordone,
  Rubens, del Sarto,
  Perugino, Guercino
5 Sala di Saturno
  Raphael ("Madonna
  della Seggiola")
6 Sala dell'Iliade

  Velázquez, Titian,
  Raphael
7 Sala della Stufa
  Frescoes by Rosselli,
  da Cortona
8 Sala dell'Educazione
  di Giove
  Caravaggio, Allori
9 Saletta da Bagno
10 Sala di Ulisse
  Raphael, Reni, Lippi
11 Sala di Prometeo
  Signorelli, Lippi
12 Corridoio delle
  Colonne
13 Sala della Giustizia
  Veronese, Titian
14 Sala di Flora
  Canova, Bronzino

15 Sala dei Putti
  Jordaens, Rubens
16 Galleria Poccetti
  Pontormo, Rubens,
  Ribera, Dughet
17 Sala della Musica
18 Sala Castognoli
19 Sala delle Allegorie
20 Sala delle Belle Arti
21 Salone d'Ercole
22 Sala dell'Aurora
23 Sala di Berenice

A Vestibolo
B Sala degli Staffieri
C Galleria delle Statue
D Sala delle Nicchie
E Sala verde
F Sala del trono

G Sala celeste
H Cappella
I Sala dei pappagalli
J Sala gialla
K Camera da letto
L Gabinetto da
  toletta
M Sala da musica
  e da lavoro
N Camera da letto
O Salotto di
  ricevimento
P Sala di Bona
Q Sala da ballo
R Sala della Fede
S Sala della Carità
T Sala della Giustizia

Palazzo Pitti: home of some of Florence's major museums

The various museums in the Palazzo Pitti have been undergoing reorganisation since 1970 so there may be some discrepancies in the listing of the exhibits.

A respected and wealthy Florentine merchant family, the Pittis were on a par with the Medicis when it came to pride and ambition. Consequently in 1447 Luca Pitti laid plans for a magnificent palace on the left bank of the Arno a little above the town. The architect Luca Fancelli was in charge of the preliminary work (1457–66), possibly based on designs by Brunelleschi. Between 1558 and 1570 Eleonora of Toledo, the wife of Cosimo I, who had acquired the palace in 1549, had it completely renovated and considerably enlarged by Bartolomeo Ammanati, who was followed by other architects, interior designers and artists.

The new owners, the Medici, and Cosimo III in particular, purchased valuable pictures to decorate the apartments. These form the basis of the Galleria Palatina. Classical and contemporary statues were also added.

The Palazzo Pitti became the residence of the country's rulers (1864–71) when Florence was the capital of a partially united Italy. In 1919 King Victor Emanuel III finally gave it to the city, which had the museums enlarged.

Architecture at its most creative can be seen in the façade of the palace with its massive ashlar stonework, high-vaulted windows and stepped stories, and in the Rondò di Bacco, the courtyard laid out in the Mannerist way by Ammanati (1558–70), looking like a grotto enlivened by "rustication". Adjoining it is the terrace of the Boboli Gardens (see Giardino di Boboli) with its fountain and statues.

Filippo Lippi:
"Madonna and Child"

Raphael:
"Madonna della Seggiola"

Raphael:
"Madonna del Granduca"

Galleria Palatina/Galleria Pitti

The entrance to the palace leads past the Cappella Palatina
(completely covered in frescoes) to the Galleria Palatina or
Galleria Pitti (first floor), where the paintings are not in
chronological order but are arranged as part of the décor as an
adjunct to the state-rooms and their costly furnishings.

The collection was begun about 1620 by Cosimo II and finally
made accessible to the public by the Italian kings.

The rooms are named after the themes of the pictures they
contain or the artists being represented.

Especially interesting are the works of Raphael (1483–1520),
Andrea del Sarto (1486–1530), Titian (1490–1576), Tintoretto
(1518–94) and Rubens (1577–1640).

The Sala di Venere containing the first paintings is reached
from the staircase via the vestibule, the Sala degli Staffieri, the
Galleria delle Statue and the Galleria delle Nicchie. This room is
part of the Appartamenti ex Reali (see entry).

Opening times
Tues.–Sat. 9 a.m.–2 p.m.,
Sun. and public holidays
9 a.m.–1 p.m.

Closed
Mon.

Sala di Venere

Among the most important paintings in the "Venus Room" are
the Pietro da Cortona ceiling, "Return of the Hunters"
(Sustermans), "The Portrait of a Lady" (Titian), "Pietro
Aretino" (Titian), "Return from the Hayfields" and "Ulysses in
the Phaecian Isle" (Rubens), "Concert" (Titian) and "Seascape
at Sunset" (Salvatore Rosa).

Peter Paul Rubens: "Holy Family"   *Titian: "Portrait of a Nobleman"*

Sala di Apollo
Among the most important paintings in the "Apollo Room" are "Mary Magdalene" and "Portrait of a Nobleman" (Titian), "Descent from the Cross" and "Holy Family" (Andrea del Sarto), "Cleopatra" (Guido Reni).

Sala di Marte
The most important paintings in the "Mars Room" include "Portrait of Luigi Cornaro" (Tintoretto), "The Four Philosophers" (Rubens), "Madonna with the Rosary" (Murillo), "Consequences of War" (Rubens), "Cardinal Ippolito de' Medici" (Titian), "Cardinal Guido Bentivoglio" (Van Dyck).

Sala di Giove
The "Jupiter Room" is decorated with frescoes by Pietro da Cortona. Important works of art: "Three Ages of Man" (ascribed to Lorenzo Lotto, Giorgione and Bellini), "Madonna with the Little Swallow" (Guercino), "John the Baptist" (Andrea del Sarto), "Descent from the Cross" (Fra Bartolommeo), "Donna Velata" i.e. Veiled Woman, or "La Fornarina", one of Raphael's finest portraits of women.

Sala di Saturno
In the "Saturn Room" the visitor should look out for "Madonna del Granduca", "Portrait of Tommaso Inghirami", "Portrait of Agnolo Doni", "Vision of Ezekiel", "Madonna with Baldachin", "Portrait of Magdalena Doni".

Sala di Apollo

Sala dell'Iliade
Of especial importance in the "Iliad Room" are "Portrait of
Philip IV of Spain" (studio of Velázquez), "La Gravida"
(Raphael), "Assumption of the Virgin" (two paintings on the
same theme by Andrea del Sarto), "Count Waldemar Christian
of Denmark" (Sustermans).

Other rooms
The tour continues through the Sala del Castagnoli ("Table of
Apollo" or "Table of the Muses" by Dupreand Papi); the Sala
delle Allegorie (with a fresco by Volterrano); the Sala delle Belle
Arti (with 17th c. Florentine paintings); the Salone d'Ercole
(with a painted ceiling by Benvenuti and a Sèvres vase); the
Sala dell'Aurora (Vasari); the Sala di Berenice; Sala di Psiche
(Salvatore Rosa); the Round Cabinet and Maria Luisa's
bathroom; the Sala della Fama (French masters), the Sala
dell'Arca; the Cappella delle Reliquie; the Sala della Musica
(dei Tamburi); the Galleria del Poccetti (Rubens, Ribera); the
Sala di Prometeo ("Madonna and Child", a masterpiece by
Filippo Lippi, "Holy Family" by Signorelli, portrait of a man by
Botticelli, "Apollo dancing with the Muses" by Peruzzi); the
Corridoio delle Colonne (Flemish masters); the Sala di Flora
("Italian Venus", marble statue by Canova); the Sala dei Putti
(Flemish masters, "The Three Graces" by Rubens); the Sala di
Ulisse ("La Madonna dell'Impannata" by Raphael and "Death
of Lucretia" by Filippino Lippi); the Saletta da Bagno; the Sala
dell'Educazione di Giove (Caravaggio, Guercino); the beautiful
Sala della Stufa ("The Four Ages of Man", wall-paintings by
Pietro da Cortona).

Sala di Flora

Appartamenti ex Reali (Former Royal Apartments)

At present closed

The collection of works of art in the Palazzo Pitti's Galleria Palatina is complemented by the Appartamenti ex Reali, the former Royal Apartments lived in by Victor Emmanuel II, Umberto I, Queen Margherita and Victor Emmanuel III. The magnificent rooms (the visitor should note the frescoes and stucco-work here, too) contain costly furniture, paintings, statues, tapestries and utensils.

Galleria d'Arte Moderna (Gallery of Modern Art)

Opening times
Tues.–Sat. 9 a.m.– 2 p.m.,
Sun. and public holidays
9 a.m.–1 p.m.

Closed
Mon.

The Gallery of Modern Art is on the second floor of the Pitti Palace. It was founded about 1860 and has been continuously expanded (by works of art transferred from other state or municipal galleries and by gifts). It gives an impressive general view of 19th and 20th c. painting in Tuscany and other parts of Italy. There are also excellent examples of 19th and 20th c. sculpture. A special section is devoted to the works of the "Macchiaioli" (the "daubers"). The representatives of this Tuscan school (including Giovanni Fattori, Silvestro Lega, Telemaco Signorini) owe their name to their anti-academic brushwork.
The final section is a collection of works by contemporary Italian painters, including Severini, Soffici, De Chirico and Morandi.

Galleria del Costume (Costume Gallery)

Opening times
Tues.–Sat. 9 a.m.–2 p.m.,
Sun. and public holidays
9 a.m.–1 p.m.

Costumes depicting the evolution of fashion from the 18th c. to 1930 are displayed in Palazzo Pitti's neo-classic Palazzina della Meridiana (entrance from the Boboli Gardens). The costumes are set amidst furnishings and paintings from the period.

Closed
Mon.

Museo degli Argenti (Silver Museum)

The ground floor and mezzanine of the Palazzo Pitti house the silver collection, which in addition to the work of silversmiths and goldsmiths also has displays of precious stones, jewelry, carved ivory and amber, painted glass and porcelain.

Opening times
Tues.–Sat. 9 a.m.–2 p.m.,
Sun. and public holidays
9 a.m.–1 p.m.

The museum's collection, founded after the First World War, is based on the silver owned by the Medici family. Other exhibits come from the Uffizi (see Palazzo e Galleria Uffizi), the Bargello (Museo Nazionale del Bargello in the Palazzo del Bargello – see entry), and the treasures of the princely archbishops of Salzburg and the kings of Italy.

Closed
Mon.

On display are 17th and 18th c. jewel caskets and reliquaries, 16th and 17th c. vases and crystalware, 16th and 17th c. tapestries, carved ivory and carved amber, the Medici's collection of jewelry, goblets, golden tableware, silver jugs and silver dishes.

Museo delle Carrozze (Coach Museum)

Like the silver collection, the Coach Museum is also on the ground floor of the Pitti Palace.

At present closed

On show are state coaches, barouches and carriages of every kind which were used by archdukes and kings in the 18th and 19th c., including the coaches of the Duke of Modena, Francesco II and King Ferdinando of Naples.

Palazzo Ricasoli   H6

The house of the Ricasoli family stands in the Piazza Goldini, the square by the Ponte alla Carraia (see entry) over the Arno where seven streets converge. (The Ricasoli family also gave its name to a winery of repute in the Chianti district.) The building used to be ascribed to Michelozzo, but it was not begun until 1480 whereas Michelozzo lived from 1369 to 1472. It was completed in the early 16th c.

Location
Piazza Goldoni 2

Buses
A, 6, 9, 11, 36, 37

Palazzo Riccardi-Manelli (Formerly Palazzo Grifoni)   K5

This imposing palace in Piazza della Santissima Annunziata (see entry) is the headquarters of the administrative authority of the province of Florence and of the Tuscany Regional Government. The three-story building with its fine dignified façade opposite the church of Santissima Annunziata (see entry) dominates the square.

Location
Piazza della Santissima
Annunziata

Buses
B, 4, 6, 34

Ugolini Grifoni, a wealthy official under Grand Duke Cosimo I, commissioned the architect Bartolomeo Ammanati to erect a palace over the top of old houses, a task which he skillfully accomplished between 1557 and 1563. The combination of red brick and predominantly light-grey stone is especially effective.

*Palazzo Rucellai   H6

The architect Bernado Rossellino built this palace between 1446 and 1451 to designs by Leon Battista Alberti. It is one of Florence's finest Renaissance mansions. It was built for

Location
Via della Vigna Nuova 18

Buses
A, 6, 11

Giovanni Rucellai, a wealthy merchant who acquired his money, refinement and standing in the 15th c.

Architect and artist, Alberti and Bernardo Rossellino, were given a free rein to show the full extent of their capabilities on the building; the prosperous merchant was only too pleased to provide the means. Their clarity of conception and breadth of execution can be seen in the finely-drawn façade with its tapering pilasters, variety of window shapes, carefully hewn blocks of ashlar and stories of gradually diminishing height. Together they created a palace that was a milestone in the architectural history of the Renaissance. Above the windows of the first floor is a stone frieze of billowing sails, the trade-mark of the Rucellai family who still own the palace today.

The Loggia dei Rucellai (columned hall), built between 1460 and 1466 opposite the palace, is also worth seeing.

Next to the church of San Pancrazio (accessible from Via della Spada) is the Cappella Rucellai (see entries) with the Edicola del Santo Sepolcro.

Palazzo della Signoria

See Palazzo Vecchio

Palazzo Spini-Ferroni   J6

Location
Piazza Santa Trinità

Buses
A, B, 6, 11, 36, 37

The largest of Florence's medieval palaces, this was built in 1289, probably to plans by Arnolfo di Cambio. Restored in 1874, its massive walls, great height and emphatic crenellation make this extensive complex on the banks of the Arno most impressive. A medieval tower and a loggia on the ground floor have disappeared.

Palazzo Strozzi   J6

Location
Piazza Strozzi

Buses
A, 6, 11, 36, 37

In the 15th c. the Strozzi family, who considered themselves just as good as the Medici, determined to outdo the ruler of Florence, Lorenzo de' Medici. Rather than erect a building that would vie with the Palazzo Medici-Riccardi (see entry) in terms of grandeur, the wealthy merchant Filippo Strozzi planned to build a house for his family that would be outstanding not for its size and splendor but for its meticulous workmanship. The Palazzo Strozzi was built between 1489 and 1538 and, in the year it was completed, it was seized by Cosimo I and withheld from the Strozzi family until 1568. Today it houses cultural institutes.

In this building the architects, Benedetto da Maiano and (after his death) Simone del Pollaiolo, known as Cronaca, achieved a combination of the greatest features of Renaissance architecture with articulation of classical beauty in the overall and detailed design and consummate craftsmanship in every aspect of the building. The impact of the façade depends on the balanced composition of the stories, the portal, the windows and the cornice as well as on the art of the stonemason evident in every one of the ashlar blocks with horizontally-aligned bosses which project progressively less towards the top of the building.

The wrought-iron work (rings in the walls for tethering horses, torch-holders and lanterns on the corners) was executed around 1500 by Niccolò Grosso, a famous blacksmith, who accepted commissions only if paid in advance.

The elegant and graceful inner courtyard by Cronaca is worth visiting.

On the ground floor there is a small museum devoted to the history of the construction of the palace, including a wooden model of the palace by da Maiano (open Mon., Weds., Fri. 4–7 p.m.).

The Galleria Strozzina (ground floor and first floor) has the Vicusseux Library and temporary exhibitions of art, both modern and from previous centuries.

Palazzo dello Strozzino   J6

In 1458, before the Palazzo Strozzi (see entry) which now stands opposite had been built, the younger branch of the Strozzi family commissioned Michelozzo to build a house which was completed between 1462 and 1465 by Giuliano da Maiano.

In 1927 the area of the inner courtyard was incorporated into the Odeon Theatre, a project of the architect Marcello Piacentini.

Location
Piazza Strozzi 2

Buses
A, 6, 11

Palazzo e Galleria degli Uffizi (Uffizi)   J6

Cosimo I de' Medici, Duke of Florence (and, after 1569, Grand Duke (Granduca) of Tuscany) moved out of the family palace (see Palazzo Medici) into the Palazzo Vecchio (see entry – also called Palazzo della Signoria) which therefore became the Palazzo Ducale (Ducal Palace). This left no room for the law-courts and governing body of Florence and plans were drawn up for offices of their own, the Uffizi, to be built adjoining the Palazzo Ducale. The foundation stone was laid in 1560. In 1565 a corridor was hastily built (in less than six months) from the Palazzo Vecchio through the Palazzo degli Uffizi and over the Ponte Vecchio to the Palazzo Pitti (see entries). The building (and the corridor) were designed and built by Vasari. Buontalenti continued to modify the Uffizi until 1586, but the loggias were glazed and made into a museum in 1581.

The Palazzo degli Uffizi encompassed the old customs building, the Zecca, where the famous coins, the "florins", were minted, and the Romanesque church of San Piero Scheraggio. This coincided with the construction of the studios and workshops where craftsmen worked with the semi-precious stones, the Pietre Dure, in which the Medici had always taken a passionate interest (see Opificio e Museo delle Pietre Dure). Rooms were also allocated for the study of the natural sciences and alchemy. In 1585–6 room was even found for a theater where the first operas in the history of music were performed.

Today the palace houses the Uffizi Galleries and the National Archives.

The Palazzo degli Uffizi is U-shaped. One wing stretches from the Palazzo Vecchio (see entry) along one side of the Piazzale degli Uffizi to the Arno. A short section then runs alongside the

Location
Piazza della Signoria/
Piazzale degli Uffizi
(entrance: Loggiato degli
Uffizi 6)

Buses
B, 13n, 19n, 23, 31, 32, 33

Opening times
Tues.–Sat. 9 a.m.–7 p.m.
Sun. and public holidays
9 a.m.–1 p.m.

Closed
Mon.

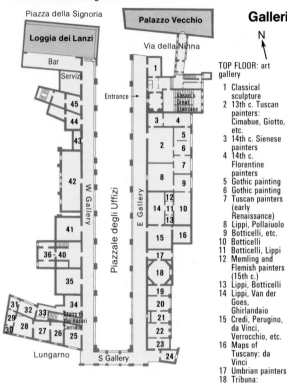

Galleria degli Uffizi

N

20 m
22 yd

TOP FLOOR: art gallery

1 Classical sculpture
2 13th c. Tuscan painters: Cimabue, Giotto, etc.
3 14th c. Sienese painters
4 14th c. Florentine painters
5 Gothic painting
6 Gothic painting
7 Tuscan painters (early Renaissance)
8 Lippi, Pollaiuolo
9 Botticelli, etc.
10 Botticelli
11 Botticelli, Lippi
12 Memling and Flemish painters (15th c.)
13 Lippi, Botticelli
14 Lippi, Van der Goes, Ghirlandaio
15 Credi, Perugino, da Vinci, Verrocchio, etc.
16 Maps of Tuscany: da Vinci
17 Umbrian painters
18 Tribuna:

FIRST FLOOR: Engravings

"Medici Venus" and Greek sculpture, paintings by Vasari, Bronzino, Pontormo
19 Perugino, Francia
20 Dürer, Cranach, Mantegna
21 Dürer, Bellini, Carpaccio, etc.
22 Holbein, David, Altdorfer
23 Correggio, Metsys
24 15th–18th c. miniatures
25 Michelangelo, Raphael, Bronzino
26 Sarto, Pontormo
27 Pontormo
28 Titian
29 Parmigianino
30 Parmigianino, Dossi
31 Dossi
32 Piombo, Bordone
33 Various 16th c. painters
34 Veronese
35 Tintoretto, Bassano, Baroccio
36–40 in course of rearrangement
41 Rubens, Van Dyck
42 Niobe Room: Roman copies in marble of Niobe and her children (original lost)
43–45 in course of rearrangement

Arno before the other (W) wing extends back along the Piazzale to the Loggia dei Lanzi (see entry). On the ground floor the Palazzo has colonnades, columns alternating with pillars where stallholders still display their wares and which from time immemorial has been animated by the bustle of the people of Florence and visitors to the city. On the upper floors are the offices and works of art.

The uniform severely articulated façades conceal an irregular interior that developed from various 14th and 16th/17th c. buildings.

It was also the first building in Europe to use cement and iron struts.

**Galleria degli Uffizi (Uffizi Gallery)

Location
Piazzale degli Uffizi/Piazza della Signoria (entrance: Loggiato degli Uffizi 6)

Buses
B, 13n, 19n, 23, 31, 32, 33

The art collection in the Uffizi was founded by the Medici, the one-time rulers of Florence and Grand Dukes of Tuscany. In the course of time it has developed into the most important art gallery in Italy and one of the best in the world with some 4000 paintings, including masterpieces by Italy's greatest 13th–18th c. artists and from other European countries. In addition there are dozens of priceless Classical sculptures as well as tapestries, drawings, jewelry, weapons, scientific instruments and archaeological finds – indicative of the unique and equally admirable patronage of the Medici.

It is only very recently that it has been possible to compile a comprehensive catalogue of the host of objects, many of which are in storage.

Before viewing the collection of paintings, the visitor is advised to see the archeological section near the entrance; here can be seen the remains of the church of Pier Scheraggio, a Romanesque building partly destroyed when the Uffizi was built.

To get to the actual collection of paintings from the Sala della Biglietteria (tickets) with frescoes by Andrea del Castagno and the "Annunciation" (1481), a masterpiece by Botticelli, the visitor can pass through the "Gabinetto dei Disegni e delle Stampe" (Engravings Room, drawings and prints; 104,000 items in storage alone); then come two vestibules with statues. After that the visitor reaches the galleries on the second floor extending right round the Piazzale degli Uffizi which are furnished with Roman marble statues and bronze figures, tapestries and rich wall-decoration.

The extent of the collection means that only the most outstanding works of art can be mentioned.

Room 2 (13th c. Tuscan school): "The Rucellai Madonna" by Duccio di Buoninsegna (c. 1285), "Madonna and Child and Four Saints" and "Madonna with Angels and Saints" by Giotto (c. 1310), "Madonna in Maestà" by Cimabue (between 1280 and 1290).

Room 3 (14th c. Sienese school): "Annunciation with Saints" by Simone Martini (1333) and "Madonna in Glory" (1340) by Pietro Lorenzetti.

Room 4 (14th c. Florentine school): "St Matthew" by Andrea Orcagna and Jacopo di Cione (1367), "Pietà" (after Giotto) and "San Nicola da Bari" by Ambrogio Lorenzetti (1332).

Rooms 5 and 6 (Later Gothic schools): "Adoration of the Magi" by Lorenzo Monaco (1420), "Crucifixion" by Agnolo Gaddi, "Madonna and Child" by Jacopo Bellini, "Adoration of the Magi" by Gentile da Fabriano, his masterpiece, and "Coronation of the Virgin" by Lorenzo Monaco (1413).

Room 7 (early 15th c. Florentine school): one section of the famous "Battle of San Romano" by Paolo Uccello (1456), portraits by Piero della Francesca (1465), "Madonna and St Anne" by Masaccio and Masolino da Panicale (1420 or 1424), "Madonna in Majesty" by Domenico Veneziano and "Madonna and Child" and "Coronation of the Virgin" by Fra Angelico (1430 and 1435).

Room 8 (Room of the two Lippis, father and son): most of the paintings by Filippo and Filippino Lippi are scenes from the life of the Virgin.

Room 9 (Pollaiolo and Botticelli Room): "Portrait of an Unknown Man" (1470) and "Judith and Holofernes" by Botticelli (1487–92), and "Virtues" by Piero del Pollaiolo and Botticelli.

Opening times
Tues.–Sat. 9 a.m.–7 p.m.;
Sun. and public holidays
9 a.m.–1 p.m.

Closed
Mon.

Titian: Venus of Urbino

Botticelli: Birth of Venus

Rooms 10–14: The main works in the room where the pictures have been rearranged (also possibly in other rooms) are "The Birth of Venus" (1486) and "La Primavera" ("Spring", 1477–8), two of Botticelli's masterpieces; other paintings by Botticelli are "Adoration of the Magi" (1475), "Pallas and the Centaur" (1485), "Madonna of the Magnificat" (1481–2), "Madonna with the Pomegranate" (1487) and "Calumny" (1494–5).
Other interesting paintings are those by Ghirlandaio, Filippino Lippi, Hans Memling (portrait), Roger van der Weyden ("Entombment") and the well-known "Portinari Triptych" by Hugo van der Goes.

Room 15 (15th c. Tuscan and Umbrian school): "Baptism of Christ" by Andrea Verrocchio (1470) and Leonardo da Vinci, works by Signorelli and Perugino, "Adoration of the Magi" by Leonardo da Vinci (1481), and "Annunciation", an early work by Leonardo da Vinci or Ghirlandaio (1470–5).

Room 17 (of the Hermaphrodite): Triptych and "Madonna delle Cave" by Andrea Mantegna, and Classical sculptures ("Hermaphrodite", "Cupid and Psyche").

Room 18 ("Tribuna"): In the centre is the "Medici Venus", the most renowned Classical marble sculpture in Florence (copy after Praxiteles); other important statues are the "Apollino" (after Praxiteles), "Arrotino" ("Scythian Sharpening a Knife", 3rd or 2nd c. B.C. Pergamon school), "Wrestlers" (Pergamon school) and "Dancing Faun" (3rd c. B.C. copy).
The walls are mainly decorated with portraits of the Medici family (Vasari, Pontormo, Andrea del Sarto, Bronzino).

Room 19: Most of the paintings in this room are by Perugino (Don Biaggio Milanesi, the monk Baldassare, Francesco delle Opere and his 'Madonna between John and Sebastian") and by Luca Signorelli ("Holy Family" and "Madonna and Child").

Room 20 (German school): This room contains works by German masters. Lucas Cranach's "Martin Luther", "Katharina von Bora", "Self Portrait", "Saint George", another "Martin Luther", "Melanchthon" and "Adam and Eve". In the style of Cranach: "Portrait of a Lady", "John I", "Ferdinand III of Saxony"; "Portrait of a Young Man" by Joos van Cleve.
Albrecht Dürer's "Madonna and Child" ("Madonna with the Pear"), "Portrait of the Father" (1490), "Adoration of the Magi" (1504), an exemplary work, "Philip and James" and the drawing "Calvary".

Room 21 (15th and early 16th c. Venetians): "Holy Allegory" by Giovanni Bellini, and "Scenes from the Life of Moses".

Room 22 (16th c. German and Flemish painters): Works by Gerard David ("Adoration of the Magi"), Hans Holbein ("Portrait of Richard Southwell") and Albrecht Altdorfer ("St Florian").

Room 23 (Correggio Room): "Madonna", "Rest on the Flight into Egypt" and "Madonna in Glory" by Correggio; also two works ascribed to Raphael.

Botticelli:
"La Primavera"

Botticelli:
"Man with Medal"

P. della Francesca:
"Duchess Battista Sforza"

Rosso Fiorentini: "Cupid Playing the Lute"

Room 24: 15th to 18th c. miniatures.

Rooms 25 and 26 (Michelangelo, Raphael and del Sarto Rooms): "The Holy Family" is the only (incomplete) panel definitely ascribed to Michelangelo. He created it between 1504 and 1505 for the wedding of Agnolo Doni and Magdalena Strozzi which is why it is also known as the Doni Tondo.
There are also works by Raphael (Portrait of Perugino), Fra Bartolommeo ("Vision of the Virgin") and Albertinelli. Masterpieces by Raphael are "Pope Leo X with Cardinals Giulio de' Medici and Luigi de' Rossi" (1518–19) and "The Madonna with the Goldfinch" (1506), also "Portrait of Francesco Maria della Rovere" and "Portrait of Julius II" (uncertain); also outstanding is Andrea del Sarto's "Madonna of the Harpies" (after the figures on the pedestal; 1517).

Room 27 (Pontormo Room): "Supper at Emmaus" and "Holy Family" by Pontormo (1525/1540).
Room 28 (Titian Room): Works by Titian in this room include his "Venus of Urbino" (1538), "Ludovico Beccadelli" (1552), "Venus and Cupid" (1560), "Eleonora Gonzaga della Rovere", "Francesco Maria, Duke of Urbino" and "Flora", one of his finest portraits of women.

Room 29: "Madonna with the Long Neck" and portrait of a man by Parmigianino.

Room 30: 16th c. Emilian schools.

Room 31 (Dosso Room): "La Fornarina" by Sebastiano del Piombo (1512) and "Head of a Youth" by Lorenzo Lotto (1505).

Room 32: Works by Sebastiano del Piombo, including "The Death of Adonis".

Passage 33 (Corridoio del Cinquecento): 16th c. Italian and foreign masters, including Clouet, Poppo, Zucchi, Amberger and Moro.

Room 34 (16th and 17th c. Venetians): "Holy Family with St Barbara", "Annunciation" and "Martyrdom of St Justina' by Veronese; portrait of a man by Tintoretto.

Room 35: "Leda", "Jacopo Sansovino", "Christ at the Well" and "The Samaritan Woman" by Tintoretto, Portrait of Francesco Maria della Rovere and "Madonna del Popolo" by Barocci.

Room 41: Portrait of Giovanni di Montfort by Antonis van Dyck. Some of Rubens' best works are here: "Henri IV at Ivry" and "Henri IV entering Paris", "Isabella Brandt" (his first wife) and "Entry of Ferdinand of Austria into Antwerp".

Rooms 43–45 are being rearranged so it is possible that works will not be found in the order given here.

Lucas Cranach: "Martin Luther"

Pontormo: "Cosimo the Elder"

Filippo Lippi: "Madonna and Child"

P. della Francesca: "Duke of Urbino"

Canaletto: Doges' Palace in Venice

Room 42 (Niobe Room): Pride of place in this room, built between 1779 and 1780, is taken by "Niobe and her Children", a Roman copy, discovered in Rome in 1583, of a 5th and 4th c. B.C. Greek original. It is the finest Classical sculpture in Florence after the Medici "Venus". In the middle is the "Medici Vase", a 2nd c. B.C. work; there are also Classical statues and paintings primarily by 18th c. artists (Canaletto).

Room 43: Flemish and Dutch painters.

Room 44: "Medusa", "Youthful Bacchus" (1589), "Sacrifice of Isaac" by Caravaggio (1590). Rembrandt's works in the Uffizi are "Self Portrait as an Old Man" (1664), "Portrait of an Old Man" (the so-called "Rabbi"; 1658 or 1666) and "Self Portrait as a Young Man" (1633–4).

Between Room 35 and Room 34 is the entrance to Vasari's "corridor" (Corridoio Vasariano) which leads over the Arno by way of the Ponte Vecchio to the Palazzo Pitti (see entries). It houses more than 1000 self portraits of Italian and foreign painters. Viewing only by prior arrangement.

The approximately 400 rooms of the National Archives in the Uffizi contain parchments and historical documents, currently undergoing reorganization.

Palazzo Vecchio e Quartieri Monumentali J/K6
(Or Palazzo della Signoria and monumental quarters)

Location
Piazza della Signoria

Buses
B, 13n, 19n, 23, 31, 32, 33

Opening times
Mon.–Fri. 9 a.m.–7 p.m.;
Sun. and public holidays
8 a.m.–1 p.m.

Closed
Sat.

The austere beauty of the city and the pride and tenacity of the people of Florence are embodied in the Palazzo Vecchio (or della Signoria) in a unique way. The city's principal palace came into existence when Florence was beginning its rise to power and greatness, was a witness to the decades of its artistic and cultural heyday and stayed on as the symbol of its glorious past. The defiant fortress-like structure of the main building serves to express the power exercised by the Florentine community from the 14th to the 16th c., while its bold and lofty tower symbolises the fierce pride of the people of Florence and the furnishings within the palace reflect their love of art.

Arnolfo di Cambio is said to have begun the building (1299–1314). Thereafter several patrons and architects (Michelozzo) were responsible for modifying the work and for the additions and alterations. At first the palace was the official residence of the Priors (Palazzo dei Priori) and of the Gonfaloniere, which made it the seat of the governing body of the Republic, the "Signoria".

Its other names, Palazzo del Popolo and Palazzo del Comune, are accounted for by the republican-democratic nature of Florence, even when it was ruled by the Medici, although they governed from their family palace, the Palazzo Medici (see entry). It was Cosimo I, Duke then Grand Duke of Tuscany, who moved into the city's principal palace in 1540, after which it was known as the Palazzo Ducale (Ducal Palace). Soon, however, he moved into the Palazzo Pitti, so the name of Palazzo Vecchio (old palace) became current. Between 1865 and 1872, during the Italian struggle for unity, it was for a while the seat of the Government, the Chamber of Deputies and the Foreign Ministry.

Exterior

On the far left of the main entrance is a copy of Donatello's Marzocco, the heraldic lion of Florence with the city's coat of arms between its paws and a copy of Donatello's bronze statue of "Judith and Holofernes" (1455–60); the original is in the Sala del Gigli (see p. 93).
On the right is a copy of Michaelangelo's "David" and a marble statue of Hercules and Cacus by Bandinelli (1533). Directly under the battlemented gallery are the coats of arms of the communes of Florence. The clock at the base of the tower dates from 1353.

Interior

The palace's exhibition rooms are on the ground, first and second floors.

Ground floor

The ground floor has three courtyards, the armoury and the great staircase leading to the upper floors. The first courtyard and the armoury are especially interesting.

Courtyard
The small inner courtyard, the "Primo Cortile", was redesigned by Michelozzo in 1470 (splendid columns!). In the centre is an elegant fountain with a putto and dolphin (1476), a copy of the original by Verrocchio which is now inside the palace. Around the top of the walls are 18 large townscapes, painted on the occasion of the wedding of Francesco de' Medici and Johanna of Austria (1565). Beneath the arcade is Perino da Vinci's marble group "Samson and the Philistine".

Armory
The armory is worth visiting as it is the only room to have survived from the 14th c. palace.

Staircase
The great staircase was the work of Vasari (1560–3).

Salone dei Cinquecento (Room of the Five Hundred)   First floor
This vast room (176 ft – 53·7 m long, 71·5 ft – 22·4 m high and 61·3 ft – 18·7 m wide) is the work of Simone del Pollaiolo, known as Cronaca (1495). The walls were once decorated with two famous paintings, Michelangelo's "Soldiers Bathing" and Leonardo's "Battle of Anghiari", but both have been lost. The ceiling is divided into 39 panels richly decorated with allegories and scenes from the history of Florence and of the Medici family.
On the left is what is known as the "Audience Room", which was reserved for receptions and official ceremonies, with niches containing statues of the Medici: Cosimo I, Pope Leo X, Giovanni delle Bande Nere, Allessandro, Pope Clement VII who was crowned by Emperor Charles V, Francesco I (by Bandinelli, de' Rossi and Caccini).
Against the opposite wall is Michelangelo's famous "Genius of Victory" ("Genio della Vittoria" – 1532–4), which was probably executed for the tomb of Pope Julius II in Rome. The statue shows the artist's supremely confident mastery in his shaping of the marble and his creative genius in the beauty and movement of the body. In the alcoves next to this are Roman statues: Ganymede, Mercury, Apollo and Bacchus.
Paintings, frescoes, statues ("Hercules" by Vincenzo de' Rossi) and tapestries complete the room's furnishings.

Quartiere di Leone X
Leo X's quarters lead off from the Salone dei Cinquecento (on the opposite side of the entrance, right). Today this is where the mayor and city council have their offices, which is why these rooms are not open to the public.

Studiolo di Francesco I de' Medici
To the right of the entrance a door leads to Francesco I's study, designed by Vasari and richly decorated with paintings, frescoes and statues. Eminent painters (Bronzino, Poppi, Tito, Naldini) and sculptors (Giambologna; 'Aeolus" or small Apollo) were employed on this "jewel casket" of Florentine late-Renaissance art.

Tesoretto
A secret staircase leads to the Tesoretto, Cosimo I's little study, with ceiling paintings by pupils of Vasari.

On the other side of the Salone dei Cinquecento (on a level with the "Audience Room") are the Ricetto (anteroom), the Sala degli Otto di Pratica and the Sala del Dugento with "Cosimo's bath".

The following rooms may be visited on the second floor: Second floor

Sala dei Gigli (Lily Room)
The Lily Room has a large fresco by Ghirlandaio (1481–5).

SECONDO PIANO

PRIMO PIANO

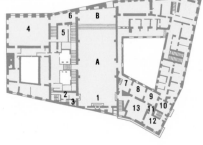

PIANTERRENO

Palazzo Vecchio Palazzo della Signoria

SECOND FLOOR (SECONDO PIANO)
1 Sala degli Gigli
2 Guardaroba
3 Cancelleria, former office of N. Machiavelli
4 Sala dell'Udienza
5 Cappella della Signoria
6 Camera di Gualdrada
7 Camera di Penelope
8 Camera di Ester o Sala da Pranzo
9 Camera delle Sabine
10 Salotto
11 Camera verde
12 Cappella di Eleonora
13 Sala degli Elementi
14 Loggiato di Saturno
15 Camera di Ercole
16 Camera di Giove
17 Camera di Cibele
18 Camera di Cerere

FIRST FLOOR (PRIMO PIANO)
A Salone dei Cinquecento
B Udienza
1 ''Il Genio della Vittoria'', by Michelangelo
2 Studiolo di Francesco I de' Medici
3 Tesoretto, Cosimo I's writing desk, by Vasari
4 Sala dei Dugento
5 Sala degli Otto di Pratica
6 Ricetto
7 Sala del Duca Cosimo I
8 Sala di Lorenzo il Magnifico
9 Sala di Cosimo il Vecchio
10 Sala di Giovanni delle Bande Nere
11 Cappella di Leone X
12 Sala di Clemente VII
13 Sala di Leone X

GROUND FLOOR (PIANTERRENO)
A Primo Cortile (courtyard)
B Camera dell'Arme
C Scalone del Vasari

Palazzo Vecchio: Florence's principal palace ▶

Cancelleria
In the Chancellery of the Secretary of the Republic stands a bust of Niccolò Machiavelli and the original of Verrocchio's "Putto and Dolphin" removed from the fountain in the courtyard.

Guardaroba
The cloakroom is fitted out with beautiful wooden presses.

Sala dell'Udienza
This Audience Room has a richly carved ceiling (by Giuliano da Maiano) and frescoes (including figures by Domenico Ghirlandaio).

Cappella della Signoria
This contains a large fresco by Ridolfo Ghirlandaio.

Quartiere di Eleonora di Toledo.
The apartments of the consort of Cosimo I, Eleonora of Toledo, who died at an early age in 1562, consist of the Camera di Gualdrada (the fresco on the bedroom ceiling shows the young Florentine woman who refused to kiss Emperor Otto IV because that was her husband's prerogative); Camera di Penelope (story of Odysseus); Camera di Ester or Dining Room (head of Apollo and fine lavabo); Salotto with interesting historical illustrations; Camera delle Sabine (ceiling painting: the Sabine women resolve the conflict between their menfolk and the Romans); Camera Verde, the "Green Room", with an adjoining study; Cappella di Eleonora (the paintings are by Bronzino).

Quartiere degli Elementi
The "Rooms of the Elements", decorated with paintings by Vasari and his pupil Gherardi (1556–66), consist of the Sala degli Elementi (allegories of Earth, Air, Fire and Water in the Mannerist style); Loggiato di Saturno (lovely view of Florence from the terrace); Camera di Ercole (scenes from the story of Hercules); Rooms of Juno, Jupiter, Cybele and Ceres and a small writing room.

"Ballatoio", tower room
From the "Ballatoio" it is possible to climb up to the tower room which affords a magnificent panoramic view of the city. The route to the top passes the Alberghettino, a prison cell, ironically christened the "little hotel", where Cosimo the Elder was incarcerated before he was sent into exile (1433) and where Savonarola was imprisoned (8–22 April 1498).

Quartiere del Mezzanino
The tour of the palace ends with a visit to the Quartiere del Mezzanino. The mezzanine, which Michelozzo created by lowering the ceilings, contains a display of works from the Collezione Loeser (paintings and sculptures by 14th and 16th c. Tuscan artists).

Palazzo dei Vescovi (Bishops' Palace)   L8

The palace, which was begun by Bishop Andrea dei Mozzi in
1295 near the church of San Miniato (see entry) and completed
by his successor Antonio d'Orso in 1320, served the Bishops of
Florence for a long time as their summer residence high above
the city, until in 1534 it was made part of the monastery of S.
Miniato. This building was subsequently also used as a military
hospital, a Jesuit college and, on occasions, a concert hall.
The popes often spent long periods in Florence. Pope Stephen
IX died here (buried in the church of Santa Reparata). His
successor, Nicholas II, had previously been Bishop of Florence,
an office which he retained.

Location
On the Monte alle Croci

Bus
13

Pazzi Chapel

See Santa Croce

Piazza di Bellosguardo

As the name suggests, there is a splendid view of Florence from
the Piazza di Bellosguardo, SW of the centre, with the Villa di
Bellosguardo and its beautiful garden. To the right of the Piazza
stands the Villa Belvedere al Saracino (built by Baccio d'Agnolo
in 1502 for Francesco Borgherini) and to the left is the Villa
dell'Ombrellino. A bust of Galileo commemorates the fact that
he lived here from 1617 to 1631.

Location
SW of city centre

Piazza del Duomo   J/K5

The Piazza del Duomo, the square around the cathedral (see
Duomo Santa Maria del Fiore), is one of the most important
sites in European art, with the cathedral, Giotto's Campanile
and the Baptistery (see Battistero).
The cathedral square, adjoined on the W by the Piazza San
Giovanni with the Archbishops' Palace (see Palazzo Arcives-
covile), is overlooked by several imposing buildings, including
the Loggia del Bigallo (see entry), the Palazzo della
Misericordia, the Palazzo dei Canonici, the Palazzo Guadagni
(see entry), the Museo dell'Opera del Duomo (see entry) and
the Palazzo Niccolini.

Location
City centre, E of station

Buses
1, 6, 7, 10, 11, 13r, 14, 17, 23,
25, 31, 32, 33

Piazza de Santa Croce   K6

In front of the church of Santa Croce (see entry) is a square
which would have been considered unusually large in the
Middle Ages. It was obviously intended for festivals and
popular assembly or as a site for the Franciscan monks to
preach their sermons. A type of football was played here as
early as the 16th c.; a commemorative plaque on the façade of
the Palazzo dell'Antella marks a boundary line.
Focal points are the 17th c. fountain on the W side of the square,
the large monument to Dante and two Palazzi.

Location
E edge of city

Buses
13r, 14, 19n, 23, 31, 32, 33

* Piazza di Santa Maria Novella

H5

Location
City centre

Buses
9, 13, 14, 17, 19, 22, 23, 36, 37

In the bustling five-sided Piazza in front of the church of Santa Maria Novella near the Loggia di San Paolo (see entries) stand two marble obelisks surmounted by bronze lilies and supported by four tortoises (By Giambologna; 1608). They mark the ends of the course of the annual chariot race, the "Palio dei Cocchi".

* Piazza della Santissima Annunziata

K5

Location
City centre, E of station

Buses
B, 1, 4, 6, 7, 10, 11, 17, 25, 34

Judged the most beautiful square in Florence, the tone of the spacious Piazza della SS. Annunziata is set by four buildings of artistic importance – the church of Santissima Annunziata (see entry) at the top, the portico by Brunelleschi of the foundling hospital, the Spedale degli Innocenti (see entry) on the right, the colonnades of the Confraternità dei Servi di Maria, the work of Antonio da Sangallo and Baccio d'Agnolo, on the left and Ammanati's Palazzo Riccardi-Manelli (see entry).

In the middle of the square are the equestrian statue of Grand Duke Ferdinand I (Giambologna's last work, completed by his pupil Tacca in 1608) and two fountains with sea-creatures in bronze, the work (1629) of Pietro Tacca from Carrara, sculptor, caster of metals and architect rolled into one, and his assistants.

▼ *Florence: Panorama of the city from the south-west*

*Piazza della Signoria con Fonte di Piazza (Neptune Fountain) J6

The Piazza della Signoria has been the political centre of the city since the 14th c. when houses belonging to Ghibelline families had to make way for the new square. The square is notable for its important buildings and statues – the Palazzo Vecchio, Palazzo degli Uffizi, Loggia dei Lanzi (see entries) and the statues by Michelangelo and Donatello (some of the originals are in the Galleria dell'Accademia, see entry).

There are also two memorials here: a small disc in the pavement, not far from the Neptune Fountain, marks the place where Savonarola and his companions Buonvicini and Maruffi were hanged and burned at the behest of Pope Alexander VI.

Near the fountain stands the equestrian statue of Cosimo I who had been elevated to the title of Grand Duke of Tuscany by Pope Leo V in 1569. The statue, by Giambologna, dates from 1594.

The most impressive monument in the square, however, is the Fonte di Piazza (del Nettuno), the Fountain of Neptune.

The Piazza della Signoria was to be decorated with a magnificent work of art for the wedding of Francesco de' Medici, son of Cosimo I, to Princess Johanna of Austria (1565), since through this marriage the Medici were rising into the ranks of the great ruling houses of Europe and Francesco even received the title of Grand Duke. Consequently a fountain which had already been begun to the left of the entrance to the Palazzo Vecchio had to be swiftly completed. Between 1563 and 1575 Bartolommeo Ammanati and his assistants made it the largest fountain in Florence, with the god Neptune, four horses and three tritons.

Location
City centre, N of the Arno

Buses
B, 19n, 23, 31, 32

The work possibly proceeded with too much haste, for the people of Florence jeered: "Ammanato, Ammanato, che bel marmo hai rovinato." ("What fine marble you have ruined!")

* Piazzale Michelangelo   L7

Location
SE of city centre

Bus
13

Florence's finest viewpoint is named after the artist who did not always receive the best of treatment from the people of Florence. It was designed by Giuseppe Poggi and laid out between 1865 and 1870. In hardly any other city in the world can well-known landmarks be as easily identified with the aid of a map as they can be here.

In the middle of the square are statues commemorating Michelangelo: bronze copies of "David" and of his four statues ("Times of the Day") for the Medici tombs in San Lorenzo (see entry).

Pinacoteca dello Spedale degli Innocenti

See Spedale degli Innocenti

Poggio a Caiano

Location
18 km (12 miles) NW

Opening times
Villa Medicea:
Tues.–Sun. 9 a.m.–1.30 p.m.;
Garden: 9 a.m.–4.30 p.m.
(until 7 p.m. in summer)

About 18 km (12 miles) NW of Florence, in the village of Poggio a Caiano, stands the Villa Medicea, generally considered to be the Medici's finest and most splendid summer residence. It was built by Giuliano da Sangallo for Lorenzo the Magnificent. The Medici loved this residence and had alterations and extensions carried out in later years.

Yet again details such as the entrance loggia, the terracotta reliefs in the entrance hall, the large drawing room with its frescoes by Andrea del Sarto, Pontormo, Franciabigio and Allori ("Cicero's return from Exile", "Caesar accepting Tribute from Egypt", "Vertunno and Pomona") testify to the artistic sensibilities of the Medici.

King Victor Emmanuel II, who lived here with his morganatic wife, the Contessa di Mirafiori, also left it fine furniture and decorations.

The villa has a lovely garden.

Ponte alla Carraia (Bridge)   H6

Location
S of Piazza Goldoni

Buses
A, 6, 9, 11, 36, 37

The second oldest bridge over the Arno collapsed several times and had to be rebuilt, as for example in 1304 when the bridge was crowded with spectators trying to watch a spectacle on the Arno, or as a result of flooding. It was built in its present form, with five arches, by Ammanati in 1559.

The Ponte alla Carraia was also blown up by German troops during the Second World War but it was possible to rebuild the bridge in its original form.

Ponte alle Grazie (Bridge)   K6/7

Location
Foot of Via de' Benci

The first bridge upstream of the Ponte Vecchio (see entry) is the Ponte alle Grazie which was built in 1237 on the orders of

Mandella, Podestà of Florence. The bridge withstood the 1333 flood but was so badly damaged in the Second World War that it had to be rebuilt in its modern form. The name of the bridge comes from a nearby chapel dedicated to the Virgin.

Buses
B, 13, 19, 23, 31, 32, 33

Ponte Santa Trinità (Bridge)   H/J6

The Ponte Santa Trinità is the most elegant bridge in Florence. It was first built in 1252 but soon collapsed. Rebuilt more solidly in stone, it was again destroyed when the Arno burst its banks in 1333 and 1557. It was built in its present form by Ammanati between 1567 and 1570 (reportedly in consultation on artistic matters with Michelangelo).
When it was blown up by German troops in 1944 the people of Florence gathered up the fragments which made it possible to rebuild it in its original form between 1955 and 1957.
On the corners of the bridge stand allegorical figures of the four seasons; they were placed here in 1608.

Location
Just S of Piazza Santa Trinità

Buses
A, B, 6, 11, 36, 37

Ponte Vecchio (Old Bridge)   J6

It is possible that the Ponte Vecchio, the "Old Bridge", at the narrowest point on the river dates back to Etruscan times. It is known for certain this is where there was a wooden bridge for the Roman consular road, the Via Cassia, to cross the Arno. On account of its age the Ponte Vecchio has undergone more repair following collapse or flooding than any other bridge in the city.

Location
City centre

Bus
B

Ponte Vecchio: the "Old Bridge" at the Arno's narrowest point

Shops and dwellings have been built on it since the 13th c. It was handy for the butchers who could throw their waste straight into the river, to the delight of the fish and those Florentines who had to keep the city clean. The number of shops increased to such an extent, however, that Grand Duke Ferdinando I decreed "for the benefit of strangers" that only goldsmiths might have shops on the bridge, a ruling that has been observed right up to the present.

In the middle of the bridge is a bust of the famous Florentine goldsmith Benvenuto Celini (1900). At first-floor level above the shops is the Corridoio Vasariano, the passage linking the Palazzo degli Uffizi to the Palazzo Pitti across the river (see entries). When it was built in the 16th c. the corridor had to be taken around the Mannelli tower on brackets since the Mannelli family refused to allow it to be built through their tower.

Porta alla Croce   M6

Location
Piazza Beccaria

Of the city's defensive walls only the Porta alla Croce, the Cross Gate, in Piazza Beccaria, built in 1284, remains. Inside is a seriously damaged fresco by Michele di Ridolfo, "Madonna and Child with St John the Baptist and St Ambrose".

Porta Romana (City Gate)   G7

Location
Via Romana

Buses
B, 38, 42

The Via Cassia, the road that led to and from Rome, passes through the Porta Romana, the Roman Gate, largest and best-preserved of Florence's city gates. Above the arch inside the gatehouse, which was built in 1326, is a fresco of the 14th c. Florentine school, "Madonna and Child and Four Saints" (Franciabigio).

Porta San Frediano (Or Porta Pisana; City Gate)   G6

Location
Borgo S. Frediano

Buses
A, 6

From the Arno a section of the old city wall leads to the Porta San Frediano. This gate is also known as Porta Pisana because it was from here that the road to Pisa left the city. This massive structure was built between 1332 and 1334, probably to designs by Andrea Pisano. The formidable doors are 43.3 ft (13.2 m) high and 10 in. (25 cm) thick.

Porta San Giorgio (City Gate)   J7

Location
Costa S. Giorgio

The Porta San Giorgio, completed in 1260, is part of the second circle of walls on the left bank of the Arno, the course of which can still be traced from the positions of the city gates of San Niccolò (see entry), San Miniato, San Giorgio and Porta Romana and San Frediano (see entries).

The interior fresco of the Madonna is by Bicci di Lorenzo; on the outside is a relief of St George.

Porta alla Croce

Porta Romana

Porta San Niccolò (City Gate)   L7

The Porta San Niccolò was equally suited for defense by land
and, in conjunction with the Zecca tower on the opposite bank
of the Arno, for sealing off the river. The tower of the bastion,
built in 1324, forms the beginning of the city wall in the E on the
left bank of the Arno.

Location
Piazza Poggi

Buses
8, 13n, 23r

Rotonda del Brunelleschi   K5
(Officially: Rotonda di Santa Maria degli Agnoli or Angeli)

The Rotonda di Santa Maria degli Agnoli (or Angeli), also
known as Rotonda del Brunelleschi, forms the nucleus of an
octagonal church which Brunelleschi began after 1433 for the
cloth-merchants' guild but never completed. The Rotonda is
thought to be the first Renaissance building to be based on a
central plan. In 1936 neighbouring buildings were demolished
with the result that the Rotonda is now free-standing.

Location
Via degli Alfani

Buses
B, 6, 34

Rucellai Chapel

See San Pancrazio

103

San Carlo dei Lombardi (San Carlo Borromeo; Church)   J6

Location
Via Calzaiuoli

Buses
B, 6, 7, 11, 19n, 23, 31, 32, 33

Opposite Orsanmichele (see entry) is the little Gothic single-naved church of San Carlo which was built between 1349 and 1404 first by Neri di Fioravante and Benci di Cione and then by Simone Talenti. It did not get its present name until the 17th c. when it was entrusted to the care of Lombards. St Carlo Borromeo was a bishop of Milan. Until then it had been dedicated to St Michael and St Anne.

San Felice (Church)   H7

Location
Piazza San Felice

Bus
B

The history of the church, which stands opposite the Palazzo Pitti (see entry), extends far back into the Middle Ages (1066). The façade, a classic example of simple yet effective Renaissance architecture, was built about 1450. The church contains works by the Giotto school ("Christ Crucified"), by the schools of Filippino Lippi (triptych), Ridolfo Ghirlandaio ("Madonna and Child"), and of Neri di Bicci (triptych) and a terracotta group from the school of Giovanni della Robbia.

*San Firenze (Church)   K6

Location
Piazza San Firenze

Buses
13n, 19n, 23, 31, 32, 33

The Baroque complex of San Firenze is in the Piazza San Firenze not far from the city's main square, the Piazza della Signoria (see entry). It was built when members of the brotherhood of priests of St Philip Neri came to Florence (c. 1640).
On the square there are two church façades with a palace between them. The church of San Filippo Neri was built by Gherardo Silvani (1633–48) on the site of an old oratory dedicated to San Fiorenzo (hence the derivation of the name Firenze).
The former church of Sant'Appolinare, together with the palace, is today the seat of the Tribunale, the judicial authority. When Florence was the country's capital before the unification of Italy the buildings were also used as the Ministry of the Interior.
These court buildings contain one of the most impressive Baroque staircases in Florence. The façades of the two churches, added to the porches in 1715, were designed by Ferdinando Ruggieri.

San Frediano in Cestello (Church)   H6

Location
Piazza di Cestello

This Carmelite church and convent were formerly known as Santa Maria degli Angeli and then became a parish church dedicated to St Frediano. The church was transformed in the 17th c. when it assumed a Baroque character, as is evidenced by its distinctive little cupola and graceful campanile.
Inside is the famous "Smiling Madonna", a 13th/14th c. Tuscan painted wooden statue.

San Gaetano (Church) J5

The finest 17th c. façade in Florence belongs to the Baroque church of San Gaetano. The original 11th c. church (San Michele Berteldi) was completely rebuilt in the early 17th c. Inside, pale figures against black stone imbue the place with a special atmosphere. In the second chapel on the left is "The Martyrdom of St Laurence" by Pietro da Cortona.
In the Cappella Antinori in the adjoining monastery is a "Christ Crucified" by Filippo Lippi.

Location
Piazza Antinori

Buses
A, 22

San Giovanni(no) dei Cavalieri (Church) K4

The name of the church of San Giovanni(no) dei Cavalieri (of the Maltese Knights of St John) changed as often as did the architects. First it was "Oratory of Mary Magdalene" as a home for "fallen" girls (1326), then "San Pier Celestino" "San Niccolò" (1533), and finally "San Giovanni Decollato" (The Beheaded John The Baptist) or "San Giovanni dei Cavalieri", the patron saint of nuns from Jerusalem who had a convent (with a fine cloister) near the church.
Inside is a "Nativity" (1435) by di Lorenzo and a "Coronation of the Virgin" by di Bicci.

Location
Via San Gallo 66/70

Buses
B, 1, 20, 25, 34

*San Giovanni degli Scolopi (Church) J5

Second in importance to John the Baptist, the patron saint of Florence is John the Evangelist. It was in his honor that the architect Ammanati began to build this church and the adjacent college for the Jesuits opposite the Palazzo Medici (see entry). However, the church was completed by the architect Alfonso Parigi the Younger in 1661. When the Jesuits were banished from Florence in 1773 the church was handed over to the Piarists (Padri Scolopi). The façade and the interior, which is richly adorned with frescoes and marble, show that on this church no expense was spared.

Location
Via Martelli/Via de' Gori

Buses
B, 1, 4, 6, 7, 10, 11, 13r, 19r, 23, 25, 31, 32, 33

San Jacopo sopr'Arno (Church) J6

From the Ponte Trinità (see entry) there is a splendid view of the little Romanesque church of San Jacopo "on the Arno" (12th c.) with its beautiful Campanile (1660). The church has a porch dating from about 1000, the only one of this period in Florence. Inside are frescoes and altarpieces painted by 18th c. Florentine artists.
Near the church, on the corner of Borgo San Jacopo and Via dello Sprone, is a lovely fountain by Buontalenti.

Location
Borgo San Jacopo 34

Buses
B, 11, 36, 37

**San Lorenzo, Cappelle Medicee, Biblioteca Mediceo-Laurenziana J5
(Church with Medici Chapel and Laurenziana Library)

San Lorenzo ranks as one of the most important art sites in the Western world. The church of St Laurence, the "Old Sacristy",

Location
Piazza San Lorenzo

105

San Lorenzo

Buses
1, 4, 6, 7, 10, 11, 13, 14, 17, 23, 25, 31, 32, 33

the "New Sacristy", the "Princes' Chapel" and the "Laurenziana Library" are works of the highest architectural importance in their own right and house priceless art treasures. It was here, in their parish church, that the Medici, unrivalled as patrons, spurred on the artists of their city – Brunelleschi, Donatello and Michelangelo – to ever greater achievements.

It is said that the church of San Lorenzo was founded by St Ambrose in 393 outside the city walls of that time. It was rebuilt in the 11th c. in the Romanesque style. It was that important exponent of Florentine Renaissance architecture, Brunelleschi, who was commissioned by the Medici (from 1419 onwards) to give it its present form. The work was completed after his death but in accordance with his plans by Antonio Manetti (1447–60). Michelangelo supplied designs (drawings and models in the Casa Buonarroti – see entry) for the façade but they were never implemented, so the bare bricks are still visible. To the right of the façade in the Piazza San Lorenzo is the monument to Giovanni delle Bande Nere (1360–1429), father of Cosimo I and founder of the ducal Medici dynasty (by Baccio Bandinelli, 1540).

Interior of the church

Brunelleschi's light, harmonious interior of the church displays the clear-cut articulation of the Renaissance architecture: a beautiful marble pavement, columns with Corinthian capitals

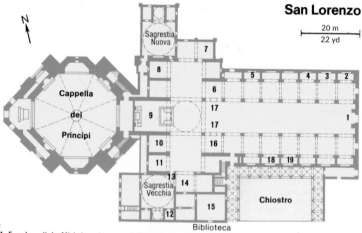

San Lorenzo

20 m
22 yd

1 Façade wall, by Michelangelo
2 "Martirio di San Sebastiano", by Empoli
3 "Sposalizio di Maria", by R. Fiorentino (1523)
4 "San Lorenzo", by N. Lapi
5 "Adorazione dei Magi", by G. Macchietti
6 Marble tabernacle, by D. da Settignano
7 Tomb of Maria Anna Carolina
8 Monument to Pietro Benvenuti

9 Cappella Maggiore
10 Wooden statue, "Madonna col Bambino" (late 14th c.)
11 Altar, by the school of Ghirlandaio
12 Marble basin, by the school of Donatello
13 Tomb of Pietro and Giovanni de' Medici, by A. del Verrocchio (1472)
14 Cappella di Ss Cosma e Damiano

15 Vestibule of the Biblioteca Mediceo-Laurenziana
16 "Martirio di San Lorenzo", by Bronzino (1565–9)
17 Bronze pulpits, by Donatello and his pupils
18 "Martirio di Sant'Arcadio e Compagni", by Sogliani
19 "Crocifisso tra la Madonna e San Giovanni" (15th and 17th c.)

supporting the broad arches, an intricate coffered ceiling with delicate rosettes. The harmonious proportions of the church's side chapels, aisles and nave denote architecture of the highest order.

At the end of the nave are two bronze pulpits by Donatello, the artist's final masterpiece (c. 1460), completed by his pupils Bartolomeo Bellano and Bertoldo di Giovanni, vividly depicting scenes from the life of Christ and the saints.

Left aisle
Above the door to the cloister is a marble balcony thought to have been designed by Donatello.
Opposite Donatello's bronze pulpit is a fresco by Agnolo Bronzino, "Martyrdom of St Laurence" (1569).

Left arm of transept
In the Cappella Martelli (left) are a diptych by Filippo Lippi, "Annunciation" (1440; on the altar), one of his major works, and a monument to Donatello (1896) by Dario Guidotti and Raffaello Romanelli.

Cloister
From the left aisle a door leads to the cloister, built in the style of Brunelleschi (1475). From here there is a magnificent view of the Campanile and the dome of Florence Cathedral (see Duomo).

Old Sacristy
The left arm of the transept leads into the Sagrestia Vecchia (old sacristy). Intended by its founder, Giovanni Bicci de' Medici, to be a burial chapel but linked with the public function of a sacristy, it was Brunelleschi's first complete architectural work (1420–8), and in its construction, articulation and proportions was to have a profound influence on European architecture.
Here, too, the impact of the building is heightened by works of art. Four medallions under the dome show scenes from the life of St John the Evangelist and four stucco reliefs in the arches depict the four Evangelists. These are all by Donatello as are the bronze doors in the apse representing martyrs and apostles in animated discourse.
On the left-hand wall is the magnificent tomb of Piero and Giovanni de' Medici (sons of Cosimo the Elder) by Andrea Verrocchio (1472). Under the marble table in the middle is the sarcophagus of Giovanni Bicci de' Medici and his wife Piccarda Bueri (the parents of Cosimo the Elder).

Cappella Maggiore (Great Chapel)
On the high altar is a "Crucifixion" by Baccio da Montelupe.

Right aisle
Opposite Donatello's bronze pulpit (in the side chapel) is a tabernacle by Desiderio da Settignano (1461).
In the last chapel but one (going towards the exit) is a painting by Rosso Fiorentino, "The Marriage of the Virgin" (1523).

Biblioteca Mediceo-Laurenziana: designed by Michelangelo

*Biblioteca Mediceo-Laurenziana (Laurentian Library)

Location
Piazza San Lorenzo 9

Opening times
Mon.–Sat. 10 a.m.–1 p.m.

Closed
Sun., public holidays

The Biblioteca Laurenziana, built on to the church of San Lorenzo and its cloister, owes its artistic importance, its architecture and its contents to the Medici family. The library was founded by Cosimo the Elder as a collection of documents and books and enlarged by Lorenzo the Magnificent. It was transferred to Rome but part of it was returned to Florence under Pope Clement VII (also a Medici), who gave orders for a building which gave the public access to the collection. Building started in 1524 to Michelangelo's designs.

Despite the difficult external conditions – it had to be built on the weak foundations of a 13th c. monastery – the library was consecrated in 1571. It shows that Michelangelo, who, after he left Florence in 1534, continued to take part in the building work by means of letters and models, was at the height of his powers as an architect. The importance of the Biblioteca Laurenziana as a work of art is due to the three-dimensional articulation of the façade, the vestibule and the reading room, the staircases, and the confident use of all the decorative elements of Renaissance architecture.

The collection of manuscripts includes important papers from Ancient Egypt and valuable manuscripts by Napoleon.

**Cappelle Medicee (Medici Chapels with the tombs of the Medici)

Location
San Lorenzo, Piazza
Madonna degli Aldobrandini

Although the Medici Chapels form part of San Lorenzo they are now run as a museum in their own right, separately from the church. They consist of the Medici family vault (Cappella dei

Cappelle Medicee: exterior ▶

San Lorenzo

Opening times
Tues.–Sat. 9 a.m.–2 p.m.;
Sun. and public holidays
9 a.m.–1 p.m.

Closed
Mon.

Cappella dei Medici

New Sacristy
(Sagrestia Nuova)

Medici) and the New Sacristy (for the oldest Medici Chapel, see
San Lorenzo, Old Sacristy).

Crypt
From the crypt, with tombs of members of the Medici family,
the visitor ascends to the Cappella dei Principi, the Chapel of
the Princes, mausoleum of the Medici grand dukes.

In 1602 Grand Duke Ferdinando I had the idea of building a
particularly splendid family vault for the Medici dynasty. The
plans were so sumptuous that the rumour went round that the
intention was to transfer the tomb of Jesus Christ from Jerusalem to Florence, for such an extravagant building could not be
intended for mortal men, not even for princes.
The final design came from Giovanni de' Medici (illegitimate
son of Cosimo I) and was put into effect by the architect
Buontalenti (1604 onwards). After his death the work was continued by Mario Nigetti (until 1640). Despite a great deal of
effort the chapel was not completed until the death in 1737 of
the last Medici to rule Florence; the huge dome, 194 ft (59m)
high but very heavy-looking, was not completed until the
19th c. The furnishings attest to the importance of the Medici
family: ceiling paintings showing scenes from the Old and
New Testaments, precious mosaics on the walls, 16 coats
of arms of Tuscan cities inlaid with semi-precious stones and,
high above, the huge coat of arms of the Medici.
Six Medici Grand Dukes are buried in the Chapel: they are
(clockwise) Cosimo I (d. 1574), Francesco I (d. 1587), Cosimo III
(d. 1723), Ferdinando I (d. 1609), Cosimo II (d. 1621) and
Ferdinando II (d. 1670). Their wall tombs and sarcophagi, executed with artistry and costly materials, were the work of highly
skilled craftsmen, but the gloomy pomp of the chapel has a
chilling air about it, an indication that the heyday of Renaissance art came and went with the 16th c. Behind the altar is the
entrance to the reliquary and treasure chapels.

The Cappella dei Principi leads into the Sagrestia Nuova, the
New Sacristy (as distinct from Brunelleschi's Old Sacristy in the
church), where Michelangelo's art reached the peak of perfection.
Cardinal Giulio de' Medici and Pope Leo X (also a Medici)
commissioned Michelangelo to build their family a funerary
chapel near the church of San Lorenzo. This chapel was the
artist's first work as an architect and to which he also applied
his twin talents as a painter and a sculptor. This can be seen in
the articulation of the internal walls, the three-dimensional
treatment given to the architectural elements, the niches and
pediments, arches and gables, both projecting and inset. The
interior with its predominant "colors" of dark grey and brilliant
white was evenly lit by the windows in the dome.
As well as his commission as architect Michelangelo was also
called upon to sculpt the tombs for members of the Medici
family. He completed only two of the tombs, however, those of
Giuliano, Duke of Nemours, and Lorenzo, Duke of Urbino.
(Lorenzo the Magnificent, his brother Giuliano, who was murdered in 1478, and Duke Alessandro, who was murdered in
1537, are also buried in the chapel but have no monuments.)
Neither Giuliano, as generalissimo of the Church of Rome
with the military commander's baton, nor Lorenzo with the

Cappelle Medicee: interior of the New Sacristy

grotesque helmet on his head (maybe a sign of his feeble-mindedness) are depicted as definite personalities, nor did the artist intend them to be. There is no satisfactory explanation either as to why the statues of "Night" (with the crescent moon and stars in her hair, and accompanied by a poppy, an owl and a mask) and "Day" (unfinished) were assigned to Giuliano, while on his tomb Lorenzo has the statues of "Dawn" and "Dusk". It is not known whether their designation is as Michelangelo intended or whether as themes they are even appropriate. What is more likely is that the artist used the exquisitely carved marble figures to express the contrasts between Life and Death, sleeping and waking, man and woman, to symbolize the Active and the Contemplative life with six statues that in the art of sculpture are unsurpassed.
Michelangelo worked on both tombs between 1524 and 1533. During the same period he also worked on the intensely emotional "Madonna and Child" (on the sarcophagus of Lorenzo the Magnificent and his brother Giuliano) but the work remains controversial; the clear face of the Madonna does not accord with the sombre and sad expression of the eyes, perhaps indicative of future sorrow.

*San Marco e Museo di San Marco

K4/5

(Church and Museum of San Marco)

The church of San Marco, built in 1299 by the Silvestrine order of monks, together with the monastery was transferred to the Dominicans of Fiesole (see entry) by Pope Eugene IV in the year of the Cathedral's consecration (1436). Thanks to the generosity of Cosimo the Elder the church was largely

Location
Piazza San Marco
Buses
B, 1, 4, 6, 7, 10, 11, 17, 20, 25, 34

San Marco: exterior (left) and cloister of St Antonino (right)

reconstructed and the monastery was completely rebuilt. The work was entrusted to the architect Michelozzo (1431–52). Giambologna added the side altars, the Chapel of St Antonino and the Salviati Chapel in 1588. The church underwent alterations by Pier Francesco Silvani in 1678 and the façade was reworked in 1780.

Interior

The single-naved church contains valuable paintings and furnishings. The following are of interest (clockwise).

Interior of the façade
In the centre is an interesting "Crucifixion" in the style of Giotto.

The Salviati Chapel (built in 1588 by Giambologna) and the Serragli Chapel are at the far end. Both contain notable paintings and sculptures.

Right
Returning to the exit along the right-hand side, the visitor will notice:
A Baroque marble door designed by Cigoli that leads to the sacristy.
A Byzantine mosaic, "Virgin in Prayer" (705–707) from the Oratory of Pope John VII in Rome.
A painting, "Madonna and Child" by Fra Bartolommeo della Porta.
The oldest part of the monastery surrounding the church houses the museum, while monks still live in the rest of the monastery buildings.

Fresco by Fra Angelico: "La Madonna della Stella" ▶

Museo di San Marco

Opening times
Tues.–Sat. 9 a.m.–2 p.m.;
Sun. and public holidays
9 a.m.–1 p.m.

Closed
Mon.

The monastery of San Marco, built in Renaissance style by Michelozzo, with its superb collection of paintings and frescoes, gives a better idea than the church of the spiritual life of the Dominicans and their interest in art.

In the late 15th and early 16th c. San Marco was the source of strong religious impulses that temporarily transformed Florence. Besides the Dominican monk Antoninus, later to become Archbishop of Florence and St Antonino, there was Savonarola, the revivalist preacher who was Prior of San Marco until he was hanged and burned in 1498.

The monastery owes its fame, however, to the Dominican monk Fra Angelico who painted the rooms of the convent between 1436 and 1445, thus leaving us today with a "natural" museum. Fra Bartolommeo, an inspired early 16th c artist, is also represented here by a number of his paintings.

The following are the works of major importance.

Ground floor

Pilgrims' hospice
Here there are panels by the Blessed Angelico from various museums in Florence, including "Madonna dei Linaioli" (1436, commissioned from Angelico by the linen weavers' guild), miniatures of the life of Jesus (1450), the famous "Deposition" (1435) and the "Last Judgment" (1430).

Cloister of St Antonino
Immediately opposite the entrance is the fresco, "St Dominic at the Foot of the Cross"; diagonally opposite the entrance, in the lunette, is the fresco, "Ecce Homo" (both by Fra Angelico).

Great Refectory
The paintings worth seeing in the Great Refectory include Fra Bartolommeo's fresco of the "Last Judgment".

Sala del Lavabo
Here there is another impressive work by Fra Bartolommeo, his large panel, "Madonna with St Anne and other Saints" (1510).

Chapter House
The whole of one wall of the chapter house, where the monks confessed and atoned for their sins, is taken up by Fra Angelico's fresco of the "Crucifixion".

Small Refectory
In the Small Refectory is a famous "Last Supper" by Ghirlandaio, similar to the one in the Ognissanti church (see entry).

First floor

On the first floor are over 40 cells which Fra Angelico and his assistants adorned with frescoes. His style is unmistakable in all the paintings and frescoes. He transforms the severity, stiffness and rigidity of the medieval saints into delicateness, softness and charm. His saints are innocent and pious yet their features are not ethereal but entirely human. Man appears transfigured, the earthly bears traces of the celestial. There is scarcely a more intimate representation of the "Annunciation" than the one by Fra Angelico (third room on the left after the stairs).

At the far end are the rooms occupied by Savonarola as Prior, containing mementoes and his portrait by Fra Bartolommeo, and the cell of St Antonino, Archbishop of Florence. The last

two cells on the side overlooking the church recall the memory of Cosimo the Elder who often came here in retreat when he was ruler of the city.
Library: The great hall of the library, the work of Michelozzo (1444), is notable for the austere beauty of its architecture and contains valuable manuscripts, missals and bibles.

San Michelino – San Michele Visdomini (Church)   K5

In the shadow of the cathedral (see Duomo Santa Maria del Fiore) is the church of San Michelino, the Vicedomini family church (hence the name San Michele Visdomini), that had to make way for the cathedral and was rebuilt a few yards away in the 14th c. (renovated in the 17th c.).
It contains altarpieces by Pontormo ("Holy Family and Saints"), Passignano, Empoli and Poppi.

Location
Via de' Servi

Buses
1, 6, 7, 10, 11, 13r, 14, 17, 19r, 23, 25, 31, 32, 33

San Miniato al Monte (Church)   L8

A visit to the church of San Miniato al Monte on the hilltop of Monte alle Croci is the easiest way to grasp the full beauty of Florence. Not only does it offer the visitor a view of the city with its incomparable skyline spread out below – but the church itself, with the classic beauty of its finely articulated 12th–13th c. marble façade and priceless works of art in the interior, is one of the most beautiful and individual Romanesque churches in Italy.

Location
Monte alle Croci

Bus
13

San Miniato al Monte: its impressively articulated façade

Mosaic in the apse: Christ with Mary and San Miniato

There was probably a church here in the time of Charlemagne; Bishop Hildebrand ordered its renovation in 1018 and by the early 13th c. both building work and decoration were largely completed. The church, together with the monastery, was originally for Benedictine nuns but between 1373 and 1552 it was used by Olivetan monks who have recently been reinstated.

Interior

The three-aisled interior is one of the most esthetically balanced in the world. The architectural features – from inlaid floor to the painted beams of the roof, the columns and vaulting, alternating green and white marble and pleasing proportions – all combine in the form of a harmonious whole.

Left aisle
In the left aisle is the Cappella del Cardinale di Portogallo (or "di San Jacopo"), one of the most richly decorated and harmonious rooms of Florentine Renaissance architecture. Its outstanding works of art are the ceiling by Luca della Robbia, the tomb of the Cardinal-Archbishop Jacobo of Lisbon (hence the name of "the Cardinal of Portugal") by Rossellino (1461), two "flying angels" by the Pollaiolo brothers (1467), Baldovinetti's panel of the "Annunciation" and his two "Prophets" (1466–7).

Campanile
In the troubled early 16th c. San Miniato's Campanile was used to defend the people of Florence against the troops of the Emperor when Michelangelo mounted two cannon here during the siege of 1530. To the right of the church stands the huge Bishops' Palace (completed in 1320 but enlarged later); amidst

the fortifications ("Fortezza") lies the vast cemetery, "Cimitero delle Porte Sante".

Nave
In the middle of the nave is the graceful chapel, the Cappella del Crocifisso, built by Michelozzo (1448) for Piero de' Medici. Its coffered ceiling is by Luca della Robbia, and Agnola Gaddi was responsible for the paintings.

Crypt
Steps on the right and the left lead down into the crypt, with six rows of beautiful columns, groined vaulting and frescoes by Taddeo Gaddi.

Presbytery and apse
The marble lattice-work (1207), the pulpit with the eagle of St John under the lectern and the (restored) apse mosaic ("Christ between the Virgin and St Minias") are among the notable features in the presbytery and apse.

Sacristy
On the S side of the raised apse is the sacristy (1387) with Spinello Aretino's masterpiece, "The Life of St Benedict". From the sacristy a door leads into the cloister which has frescoes by Andrea del Castagno and Paolo Uccello.

San Niccolò sopr'Arno (Church)   K7

An aedicula (built-up altar) in the style of Michelozzo and a lively fresco, "Madonna della Cintola" by Piero del Pollaiolo (1450) in the sacristy are the principal art treasures of the church of San Niccolò sopr'Arno which was built in the 12th c., transformed in the 14th c. and restored in the 16th c.

Location
Via San Niccolò

Buses
B, 13n, 23r

San Pancrazio e Cappella Rucellai   H6
(Former Church and Rucellai Chapel)

The former church of San Pancrazio (now occupied by national institutions) is worth seeing for its beautiful 14th c. façade and for architectural features indicative of the work of the architect Alberti.
Next to it is the Cappella Rucellai in which Leon Battista Alberti was commissioned about the year 1467 by Giovanni Rucellai to build a most unusual sepulchre which he modeled on the Holy Sepulchre in Jerusalem.

Location
Via della Spada

San Salvatore al Monte (Or San Francesco al Monte; Church)   L7

The church of San Salvatore al Monte (or San Francesco al Monte) tends to get overlooked because of the nearby church of San Miniato (see entry) but the church that Michelangelo called "la bella villanella" ("the beautiful country lass") is worth visiting for its outstanding clearcut architecture both inside and out. This is mainly the work of Cronaca (from 1499), who had considerable difficulties to overcome. Because of the steepness of the site building could proceed only by making use of retaining walls.

Location
Above Piazzale
Michelangelo, Viale Galileo

Bus
13

San Simone (Church) K6

Location
Piazza San Simone,
Via Isola della
Stinche

Buses
13r, 14, 19n, 23, 31, 32, 33

Restoration work after the 1966 floods revealed the extent of the treasures that the little church of San Simone had to offer. Founded in the 12th c. and completely transformed in the 17th c. by Silvani it has extremely elegant architecture and valuable frescoes and paintings that had almost been forgotten, including a "St Peter in Majesty" ascribed to the "Master of St Cecilia" ("Maestro della S. Cecilia").

Sant'Ambrogio (Church) L6

Location
Piazza Sant'Ambrogio

St Ambrose is one of the oldest churches in Florence. The building was transformed at the end of the 13th c. and restored several times during the following centuries; the neo-Gothic façade was added in 1887.

The single-naved church contains the tombs of famous Renaissance artists, including Cronaca (d. 1580), Mino da Fiesole (d. 1484) and Verrocchio (d. 1488).

It is furnished with notable paintings and frescoes, among them the "Madonna del Latte" by Nardo di Cione, a triptych by Bicci di Lorenzo and Cosimo Rosselli's fresco of a "Procession".

A marble tabernacle by Mino da Fiesole (1481–3) in the Cappella del Miracolo (Chapel of the Miracle) depicts the event after which the chapel is named. In 1230 a priest failed to dry the chalice properly; the next morning, it is said, the wine had changed into blood.

**Santa Croce con Cappella dei Pazzi e Museo dell'Opera di Santa Croce K/L6
(Church of Santa Croce with Pazzi Chapel and Santa Croce Museum)

Location
Piazza Santa Croce

Buses
13r, 14, 19n, 23, 31, 32, 33

"Santa Croce is a pantheon of the most dignified kind. The church has a serious and a gloomy solemnity, indeed it is a huge mortuary that no thinking person will enter without reverence", wrote Ferdinand Gregorovius, a German who travelled widely in Italy in the 19th c. It is a feeling shared by the visitor on approaching the church and entering its vast interior (photo on p. 119).

The largest and most beautiful of the Franciscan churches, Santa Croce was rebuilt in 1294 on the site of a chapel founded by St Francis of Assisi (possibly by Arnolfo di Cambio) and dedicated in 1443 in the presence of Pope Eugene IV. The façade, articulated in multicolored marble, and the Campanile date from the 19th c.

Interior

Despite additions and restoration work the church, which has always been Franciscan, has retained the character of a medieval Gothic basilica. With its tombs and monuments (276 tombstones set in the floor) and many important works of art, it is one of the finest buildings in Italy and its importance is emphasised by its impressive size. It is 378·61 ft (115·43 m) long, the nave is 125.39 ft (38.23 m) wide and the transept 241·87 ft (73·74 m) wide.

View of the basilica of Santa Croce ▶

The aisled interior with an open painted timber ceiling, octagonal columns supporting broad arches and stained-glass windows (placed there between 1320 and 1450) provides a solemn setting not only for the works of art but also for the services and sermons of the Franciscan monks.

Walking round the church in a clockwise direction the visitor should make a point of seeing the following:

N aisle

Opposite the first pillar is the tomb of the famous scientist Galileo Galilei (by Giulio Foggini). The monument to Carlo Marsuppini (by Desiderio da Settignano), one of the finest 15th c. monuments, is on the right of the side door.

N transept

On the left is the interesting monument to the Florentine composer Luigi Cherubini (d. 1842).

The Cappella Bardi in the centre contains Donatello's "Christ Crucified" which was criticized by Brunelleschi who maintained that Donatella had hung a peasant on the Cross. Brunelleschi himself created a more beautiful Crucifixion – or so he hoped – for Santa Maria Novella (see entry).

The N transept is rounded off by five chapels along the E wall. The Cappella Bardi di Vernio has wall frescoes with scenes from the life of St Sylvester (1340; by Maso di Banco); the frescoes in the burial recesses are by Maso di Banco and Taddeo Gaddi.

The Cappella Tosinghi-Spinelli has interesting stained-glass windows by the school of Giotto.

Apse

The apse is completely covered with frescoes. The frescoes in the vault are by Agnolo Gaddi (1380) and show the "Risen Christ, the Evangelists and St Francis". The wall frescoes, by Gaddi and his assistants, are of the Legend of the Cross.

S transept

The S transept also has five chapels along its E wall. The Cappella Bardi is notable for Giotto's frescoes representing the history of St Francis, which are numbered among Giotto's most mature and important works.

There are also remarkable frescoes by Giotto in the adjacent Cappella Peruzzi of scenes from the life of St John the Evangelist (right-hand wall) and of St John the Baptist (left-hand wall). These were particularly admired by the Renaissance painters and closely studied by Masaccio and Michelangelo.

In the last chapel on the left, the Cappella Velluti, are some damaged frescoes by a pupil of Cimabue ("Archangel Michael") and Giotto's "Coronation of the Virgin".

The door leads into the sacristy.

At the end of the transept is the Cappella Baroncelli with the family tomb (1328). The frescoes of the prophets at the entrance and the frescoes of the Life of the Virgin on the walls of the chapel are the greatest works of Taddeo Gaddi, one of Giotto's pupils.

In the adjoining Cappella Castellani there are important frescoes (Lives of the Saints) by Angelo Gaddi and his pupils and a beautiful tabernacle by Mino da Fiesole.

Sacristy
The doorway (by Michelozzo) gives on to a corridor, also by
Michelozzo, which leads to the Sacristy. This contains fine
Renaissance cabinets and a "Crucifixion" by Taddeo Gaddi.
At the back of the Sacristy is the 14th c. Cappella Rinuccini,
covered with frescoes by Giovanni da Milano. At the end of the
sacristy corridor is the Cappella del Noviziato (or dei Medici)
which Michelozzo built for Cosimo the Elder in 1445. The altarpiece in terracotta, "Madonna and Child" (1480), is by Andrea
della Robbia.

On the way back to the entrance can be seen:

S aisle
The tomb of the composer Gioacchino Rossini (d. 1868) and
that of the Florentine politician Leonardo Bruni (d. 1444) by
Bernardo Rossellino, the first Renaissance tomb in Florence. In
a recess is the delicate relief of the Annunciation by Donatello
(1435).
About half-way along the aisle is the tomb of Niccolò Machiavelli (d. 1527), the great historian and politician, by Spinazzi
(1787).
On the fifth pillar is the octagonal marble pulpit by Benedetto
da Maiano (1472–6) with scenes from the life of St Francis and
allegorical figures. Nearer the door is the monumental cenotaph of Dante (1829), Florence's tribute to the memory of the
poet it had sent into exile and who died in Ravenna in 1321.
On the pillar nearest the door, above the stoup, is a relief by
Antonio Rossellino, "Madonna del Latte" (1478) and, in front,
the Tomb of Michelangelo (d. 1564) by Vasari (1570).

On the right of the church is the entrance to the late 14th/early   Convent of Santa Croce
15th c. conventual buildings of Santa Croce.

First cloister
This cloister was flooded in 1966 to a depth of 19·2 ft (5·85 m)
which meant that restoration work was necessary.

Pazzi Chapel (see below)

Museo dell'Opera di S. Croce (see p. 122)

Great Cloister
This was designed by Brunelleschi and built after his death.

*Capella dei Pazzi (Pazzi Chapel)

The Pazzi Chapel is an independent complex within the church
and convent of Santa Croce. It owes its fame to the architectural
genius of Brunelleschi. He spent the period from 1430 (or 1443)
until his death in 1446 working on this classic early-Renais-
sance building for Andrea de' Pazzi. It was to be the funerary
chapel of the Pazzi family and the chapter-house of the Franciscan monks of Santa Croce.

First Cloister
The view from the first cloister of the monastery of Santa Croce
reveals the harmony of the chapel exterior with its colonnade

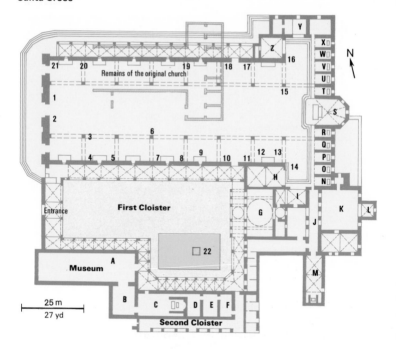

Santa Croce

1 Monument to Gino Capponi, by A. Bortone (1884)
2 Monument to G. B. Niccolini, by P. Fedi (1883)
3 "Madonna del Latte", relief, by A. Rossellino
4 Tomb of Michelangelo, by Vasari (1570)
5 Cenotaph of Dante Alighieri, by S. Rica (1829)
6 Marble pulpit, by B. da Maiano (1472–6)
7 Tomb of Vittorio Alfieri, by Canova (1810)
8 Tomb of Niccolò Machiavelli, by Spinazzi (1787)
9 "Gesù nell'Orto", by Andrea del Minga
10 Donatello's relief, "Annunciation" (1435)
11 Tomb of Leonardo Bruni
12 Tomb of Gioacchino Rossini, by G. Cassioli
13 Tomb of Ugo Foscolo
14 Tomb of Prince Corsini

15 Monument to Leon Battista Alberti, by L. Bartolini
16 Monument to Luigi Cherubini, by O. Fantacchiotti
17 Monument to Carlo Marsuppini, by D. da Settignano
18 Monument to Vittorio Fossombroni, by Bartolini
19 "Pietà", by Bronzino
20 Tomb of Galileo Galilei, by G. Foggini
21 Frescoes of saints (15th c.)
22 Marble statue "Il Padre eterno", by Bandinelli (1549)
A Room I of the Museum, former refectory
B Room II of the Museum, former Small Refectory
C Room III of the Museum, former Cappella Canigiani
D–F Rooms IV–VI of the Museum, with important paintings
G Cappella de' Pazzi, by Brunelleschi

H Cappella Castellani
I Cappella Baroncelli, with frescoes by T. Gaddi
J Corridoio della Sagrestia
K Sagrestia
L Cappella Rinuccini
M Cappella del noviziato o dei Medici, by Michelozzo (1445)
N Cappella Velluti
O Cappella Calderini
P Cappella Giugni
Q Cappella Peruzzi, with frescoes by Giotto
R Cappella Bardi, with frescoes by Giotto
S Cappella Maggiore with high altar
T Cappella Tosinghi/Spinelli
U Cappella Capponi
V Cappella Ricasoli
W Cappella Pulci e Beraldi
X Cappella Bardi di Vernio
Y Cappella Bardi with Crucifix by Donatello
Z Cappella Salviati

Interior of the Gothic basilica

and cupola. The architrave of the porch is adorned with a frieze of small medallions bearing the heads of angels (Desiderio da Settignano) and the cupola has beautiful rosettes by Luca della Robbia who also carved the "Relief of St Andrew" (1445) above the wooden doors (by Giuliano da Sangallo; 1470–8).

Interior

The interior, clearly articulated by pilasters, indentations, curvatures and barrel vault, gives the impression of uniformity, although the presence of the chancel means that the chapel is not rectangular. The four terracotta medallions in the spandrels, showing the seated Evangelists, are by Luca della Robbia, as are the twelve roundels of the Apostles (white ceramic on a blue ground).

* Museo dell'Opera di Santa Croce (Santa Croce Museum)

The museum is housed in the refectory of the monastery of Santa Croce. The particularly serious damage it suffered in the 1966 floods could only be put right by slow and painstaking restoration of the paintings, frescoes and statues.

Among the most important works of art are Taddeo Gaddi's huge (1291 sq. ft – 120 sq. m) "Last Supper", his "Entombment" and other pictures of the saints.

Other notable works include a "Crucifixion" by Cimabue, one of his later masterpieces, unfortunately seriously damaged in 1966 but which has meanwhile been restored, a bronze statue by Donatello, "St Louis" (1423), a fresco by Domenico Veneziano, "St John the Baptist and St Francis", Maso di Banco's "Coronation of the Virgin", and "Stigmata", a terracotta by Andrea della Robbia.

Opening times
Mon., Tues., Thurs.–Sun.
9 a.m.–12.30 p.m. and
2.30–6.30 p.m.
(Oct.–Feb. 3–5 p.m.)

Closed
Wed.

Santa Felicità (Church)   J6

Location
Piazza Santa Felicità

The church of Santa Felicità was built over an early Christian cemetery, rebuilt in the 11th and 14th c. and completely transformed in the 18th c. However, the porch and Vasari's "corridor", which passes through here on its way between the Palazzo degli Uffizi (see entry) and the Palazzo Pitti (see entry), were retained.

Interior

Above the entrance door is the box pew for the Grand Dukes who attended the services here.
To the right of the entrance in the Cappella Capponi can be found the church's most important works of art, two masterpieces by Pontormo (1526–8), "Entombment of Christ" and "Annunciation". The chapel was built by Brunelleschi for the Barbadori family.
The monastery belonging to the church is also of architectural interest (chapter-house).

Santa Lucia dei Magnoli (Church)   J/K7

Location
Via dei Bardi

Buses
B, 13n, 23r

The little church of Santa Lucia dei Magnoli is nicknamed "fra le rovinate" ("amidst the ruins") because the boulders on the hill were a danger to the houses surrounding it. It houses a beautiful panel by Lorenzetti of "Santa Lucia" painted on a gold ground.

Santa Margherita a Montici (Church)

Location
Via Pian dei Giullari, 2½ miles (4 km) S of the Porta San Giorgio

The partly medieval church of Santa Margherita a Montici in the lovely Tuscan hills S of Florence (beyond Pian dei Giullari) has several fine works of art: the panels "Madonna" and "Santa Margherita" by the Master of St Cecilia (early 14th c.),

▼ Fresco by Masaccio in the Cappella Brancacci: The Tribute Money

"Madonna della Cintola" by Piero del Pollaiolo (1450), an altar in the style of Michelozzo, and finely worked 15th c. liturgical vestments.

Bus
38

Santa Margherita de' Ricci (Church)   K6

In the centre of the city stands the church of Santa Margherita in Santa Maria de' Ricci or della Madonna de' Ricci which owes its name and its existence (1508) to the miraculous picture of the "Madonna de' Ricci" (c. 1300) on the high altar. Santa Margherita was the parish church of some well-known Florentine families.

Location
Via del Corso 6

Buses
14, 19n, 23, 31, 32, 33

---

* Santa Maria del Carmine e Cappella Brancacci   G/H6
(Church and Brancacci Chapel)

The large church stands in the Piazza of the same name in a busy working-class quarter of Florence. The church, begun in 1268, was not completed until 1476, as can be seen from the fact that there are both Romanesque and Gothic elements along the sides. Transformed in the 16th and 17th c., it was so badly damaged by fire in 1771 that it had to be rebuilt (by Ruggieri and Mannaioni, until 1782). The ground plan of the church is a Latin cross with a single nave flanked by various chapels. It is adjoined on the right by a cloister built in the early 17th c.

The church is principally famed for the Brancacci Chapel which houses frescoes by Masaccio (end of the right arm of the transept) and for the Baroque Cappella Corsini by Pierfrancesco Silvani (1675–83; left arm of transept), with, in the dome, a fresco of the "Apotheosis of St Andrea Corsini" by Luca Giordano (1682). The chapel contains the tombs of Neri and Pietro Corsini with three high-reliefs in marble by Giovanni Battista Foggini.

Location
Piazza del Carmine

Buses
6, 11, 36, 37

*Cappella Brancacci (Brancacci Chapel)

Location
Piazza del Carmine

In 1428 Felice Brancacci, a wealthy Florentine merchant and politician, commissioned painters, principally Masaccio and Masolino, to decorate the Brancacci family chapel with frescoes which represented an important stage in the development of European painting. In his frescoes Masaccio took art beyond the richness of form and color of the medieval Gothic and developed the ideas initiated by the famous painter Giotto.

Major Renaissance artists studied the works in the Brancacci Chapel on account of their confidence in the use of perspective, the austere realism of the characters depicted, the subtle characterisation of the faces, the freedom and intensity of expression.

Recently the frescoes, which had been considered disfigured by various attempts at restoration, have been restored to their original coloration.

The themes of the frescoes are (top row, from left to right): Expulsion of Adam and Eve from Paradise, The Tribute Money (both masterpieces by Masaccio); St Peter Preaching; Peter Baptising the Neophytes; Peter and John Healing the Lame and Raising Tabitha; The Temptation of Adam and Eve.

Bottom row: Peter Visited by Paul in Prison; Peter Raising the Son of Theophilus; Peter Preaching; Peter (with John) Healing the Sick; Peter and John Distributing Alms; Crucifixion of Peter; Peter and Paul before the Proconsul; Release of Peter from Prison.

Michelangelo is said to have become so enraged during an argument on the steps of the church while discussing these pictures that he got his nose broken in the ensuing fisticuffs.

Santa Maria dell'Impruneta (Church)

Location
Impruneta, 8 miles
(13 km) S

The 11th c. basilica stands in the little town of Impruneta which nestles among the hills of Tuscany. It was rebuilt in the 14th and 15th c. and surrounded by walls and towers. The church was severely damaged during the Second World War (photo opposite).

Of interest inside are two richly decorated aediculae by Michelozzo (1453–6), similar to the one in the church of Santissima Annunziata (see entry) in Florence, the Cappella della Croce with an altarpiece by Luca della Robbia, and the Cappella della Madonna, also decorated with works by Luca della Robbia.

The little town of Impruneta is well-known for its pottery and ceramics. The annual Fiera di San Luca is celebrated in October.

*Santa Maria Maddalena dei Pazzi, K5
Convento di S. Maria Maddalena (Church and Convent)

Location
Borgo Pinti 58

Buses
6, 13r, 14, 19r, 23, 31, 32, 33, 34

Maria Maddalena, a member of the famous Florentine Pazzi family, was canonised in 1669. The 13th c. complex of church and Benedictine convent, already transformed two centuries earlier by Giuliano da Sangallo (1480–92), was enlarged in her honor, which is why the forecourt of the church is in the

Santa Maria dell'Impruneta

Santa Maria dei Pazzi: Benedictine church

harmonious style of the second half of the 15th c. and yet there are Baroque elements in other sections of the church and the convent.

In the chapels are some valuable paintings by 15th and 16th c. artists (e.g. Portelli and Giordano).

Convento di Santa Maria Maddalena

Opening times
Daily 9 a.m.–noon,
5–7 p.m. (ring if closed)

In the chapter-house of the convent adjoining the church is one of Perugino's finest frescoes, dating from between 1493 and 1496, his most creative period: Christ on the Cross and Mary Magdalene, St Bernard and Mary, St John and Benedict, Christ on the Cross Helping St Bernard.

In the background the landscape is recognizably that of Perugino's native Umbria (Perugia).

The convent's refectory is today part of a Carabinieri barracks; Sangallo's cloister belongs to the Liceo Michelangelo. Most of the damage caused by the 1966 flooding has been repaired.

Santa Maria Maggiore (Church)   J5

Location
Via de' Cerretani

Buses
B, 1, 4, 6, 7, 10, 11, 14, 17,
19, 23, 31, 32

Not far from the Baptistery (see Battistero), in Via de' Cerretani, is one of the oldest churches in Florence, which was certainly built before the 11th c. and was rebuilt in the second half of the 13th c. (1912–13 carefully restored). The old bell-tower is still indicative of the lower level of the Romanesque church; high up in the wall is "Bertha", a late-Romanesque bust of a woman. Above the church portal is the "Madonna and Child" of the 14th c. Pisan school (copy).

The outstanding features of the aisled Gothic interior with its square pillars and fine paintings and statues are the "Madonna in Majesty with Child" (also known as "Madonna del Carmelo") and a colored gilded wooden relief. The relief shows the artist's skill not only as a sculptor but also as a painter (possibly Coppo di Marcovaldo, 13th c.).

Santa Maria Novella (Church)   H5

Location
Piazza di Santa Maria Novella

Buses
9, 13, 14, 17, 19, 22, 23, 36,
37

Opening times
Daily 7–11.30 a.m.
and 3.30–6 p.m.

One of the most important churches in Florence, the Dominican church of Santa Maria Novella was built in 1246 on the site of a 10th c. oratory (Santa Maria delle Vigne) and continually enlarged between the 11th and the 14th c. by various architects (essentially completed about 1360).

Like the Franciscan church of Santa Croce (see entry), the approach to the main building is across a large square (see Piazza di Santa Maria Novella). Here the façade is articulated by colored marble. It was added between 1456 and 1470 by Leon Battista Alberti on the orders of Giovanni Rucellai (whose family crest, the billowing sails, form the architrave half way up). The architect gave it its distinctive shape by combining Romanesque-Gothic and Renaissance styles (portal, pillars on either side, design of the upper section).

To the right of the church is an old cemetery.

Interior

The interior of the church displays a harmonious balance between soaring Gothic shapes and the extensive uniform nave

Santa Maria Novello: one of the most important Florentine churches

which appears even longer than it is (325·5 ft – 99·2 m) because the bays decrease in width from 49·2 ft (15 m) down to 37·4 ft (11·4 m) as they approach the altar. The width of 93·2 ft (28·4 m) (201·94 ft – 61·4 m in the transept) lends the Gothic interior an air of solidly based integrity.

Walking clockwise round the church the visitor can see the following important works of art:

Entrance
In the lunette above the portal is a fresco of the "Nativity" (after Filippo Lippi); in the rose-window, the oldest in Florence, the "Coronation of the Virgin".

Left aisle
On the second pillar is a marble pulpit by Buggiano from designs by Brunelleschi. On the third altar is the "Trinity", a fresco by Masaccio (1427), considered to be one of his finest works on account of its intensity of expression and perfect perspective.

Sacristy
A door leads into the sacristy which contains a marble lavabo (Giovanni della Robbia) and a "Crucifixion" by Giotto (above the door).

Left arm of the transept
Nardo di Cione painted the frescoes (based on Dante's "Divine Comedy") in the raised Cappella Strozzi in 1357. The chapel also contains Andrea Orcagna's altarpiece, "Redeemer and Saints".

A striking feature of the Cappella Gaddi is Bronzino's painting above the altar of "Christ raising the Daughter of Jairus".
In the adjacent Cappella Gondo is the celebrated wooden crucifix (between 1410 and 1425) carved by Brunelleschi in response to Donatello's crucifix in Santa Croce (see entry).

Apse

The apse was completely covered in frescoes by Domenico Ghirlandaio and his assistants (scenes from the life of John the Baptist and the Virgin). The bronze crucifix is by Giambologna.

Right arm of the transept

This also has two chapels on the left-hand side. The Cappella di Filippo Strozzi, the church's principal founder, is decorated with frescoes by Filippino Lippi (1497–1502). The Cappella dei Bardi houses Vasari's "Rosary Madonna" (1570).
At the end of the transept is the Cappella Rucellai with the bronze plate marking the grave of the Dominican-General Dati by Lorenzo Ghiberti (1423) and a marble statue of "Madonna and Child" by Nini Pisano. Nearby is the tomb of Joseph, Patriarch of Constantinople, who died here in 1440 after the Council of Florence.

Right aisle

Here a door leads into the Cappella della Pura with the miraculous picture of "Madonna and Child and St Catherine". Centered around this picture is the legend that in 1472 the Virgin, speaking from out of the picture, told two grubby children that they needed to wash themselves, an event much appreciated by Florentine mothers in bringing up their children. The chapel leads into the old cemetery.
Nearer the entrance are the tomb of the Beata Villana by Rossellino (1451) and the side altar with Macchietti's "Martyrdom of St Laurence" (1573).

Cloisters and monastery chapels

A visit to Santa Maria Novella should also include the cloisters and the adjoining chapels of the former monastery of Santa Maria Novella (entrance to the left of the façade).

"Chiostro Verde"

The name "Green Cloister" refers to the green tones of frescoes by Paolo Uccello of scenes from the Old Testament. These range from the creation of the animals and the Fall of Man (c. 1430); the compelling representation of the Flood was carried out twenty years later.

Refectory

The liturgical vessels, vestments embroidered with silver thread and the golden reliquaries date from the 14th and 17th c.

Great Cloister

From here one can visit the Cappella dei Papi on the first floor which has frescoes by Pontormo.

Cappellone degli Spagnoli

The "Spanish Chapel" was built after 1340 by Jacopo Talenti as the chapter-house of the Dominican monastery and assigned in 1540 by Eleonora of Toledo, wife of Cosimo I, to her Spanish retainers (hence the name) as a place of worship. Its frescoes are among 14th c. Italy's greatest paintings.

Andrea da Firenze (Bonaiuti) was given the theme for his paintings – "the Dominican Order and the new open path to Salvation" – by Prior Jacopo Passavanti, and combined scenes from the Scriptures, legends of saints and allegories of the Humanities.

These paintings serve as a tribute to the culture of the 14th c. in a similar way to Raphael's celebration of 16th c. culture in his Stanze frescoes in the Vatican.

Chiostrino dei Morti
The tour ends with a visit to the "Little Cloister of the Dead" with the Strozzi funerary chapel (Cappella funeraria degli Strozzi).

---

* Santa Trinità (Church) J6

The fondness of the Florentines for the church of Santa Trinità is due mainly to its venerable age. As early as the 11th c. there was a church here which was rebuilt in the 13th c. (probably by Nicola Pisano) as the first Gothic church in Florence. It was rebuilt once again in the second half of the 14th c., this time by Neri di Fioravante. The Baroque façade by Buontalenti (1593–4) is therefore in complete contrast to the soaring style of the Gothic interior.

Location
Piazza Santa Trinità

Buses
A, B, 6, 11

It has many notable works of art (here listed clockwise):

Interior

Left aisle
In the third chapel an "Annunciation" on a gold ground by Neri di Bicci and the tomb of Giuliano Davanzati (d. 1444), an early Christian sarcophagus with high reliefs; in the fifth chapel Mary Magdalene in wood by Desiderio da Settignano and Benedetto da Maiano (1464–5).

Left arm of the transept
In the left arm of the transept is the marble tomb of Bishop Benozzi Federighi (1455–6), one of Luca della Robbia's finest works.

Right arm of the transept
In the right arm of the transept the Cappella Sassetti has celebrated frescoes by Domenico Ghirlandaio (1483–6) of the "Life of St Francis" (including the famous "Confirmation of the Rule of the Order") into which the artist incorporated contemporary personalities and buildings such as Lorenzo the Magnificent, Ghirlandaio himself, hand on hip, and the Piazza della Signoria and Piazza della Trinità. The altarpiece, "Adoration of the Shepherds" is also by Ghirlandaio (1485).

Sacristy
In the sacristy is the tomb of Onofrio Strozzi by Piero di Niccolò Lamberti (1421).

Right aisle
There is a cycle of frescoes by Lorenzo Monaco in the Cappella Salimbeni and a 14th c. "Crucifixion" on panel in the chapel nearest the entrance.

Nave
Stairs in the middle of the nave lead down to the old Romanesque church below.

*Santi Apostoli (Church)   J6

Location
Borgo Santi Apostoli

Bus
B

According to an inscription in Latin (on the left of the façade) the "Church of the Holy Apostles" was founded by Charlemagne and dedicated by Archbishop Turpinus. All that is known for certain is that the church was in existence at the end of the 11th c. and was rebuilt in the 15th and 16th c. (restored between 1930 and 1938). Benedetto da Rovezzano added a fine portal to the Romanesque façade in the early 16th c.

The columns of green marble from Prato with composite capitals (the first two from the nearby Roman baths) which separate the aisles from the nave constitute a striking feature of the interior. The church and its works of art were severely damaged in the 1966 floods.

Particularly noteworthy are, in the left aisle, a large terracotta tabernacle by Giovanni della Robbia (presbytery) and the tomb of Oddo Altaviti by Benedetto da Rovezzano (1507); and, in the right aisle, a panel by Vasari "Immaculate Conception" (1541, third chapel).

**Santissima Annunziata (Church of the Annunciation)   K5

Location
Piazza della SS. Annunziata

Buses
B, 1, 4, 6, 7, 10, 11, 17, 25

Whereas the Cathedral (see Duomo Santa Maria del Fiore) serves as the ecclesiastical-religious centre of Florence and the Palazzo Vecchio (or Palazzo della Signoria; see Palazzo Vecchio) is the secular-political centre, it is, quite rightly, the square and church of Santissima Annunziata that constitute the intellectual focal point of the city. Clustered around the square are the Spedale degli Innocenti (see entry) and the Pinacoteca dello Spedale, Santa Maria degli Innocenti, the nearby university with its various faculties, the Museo di San Marco (see San Marco), the Galleria dell'Accademia (see entry) and the Accademia delle Belle Arti.

The church of the Annunziata, founded about 1250 as an oratory for the Servite Order and completely rebuilt between 1444 and 1481 by Michelozzo, is an architectural masterpiece, not least because of the unusual ground plan for the church and its monastry (nave with side chapels and a large round choir chapel in front, all with adjoining structures), while the church also houses many superb works of art.

Exterior

Portico

Four doors open out of the seven-arched portico which is supported by columns with elegant Corinthian capitals.

The door on the left leads past the Sagrestia della Madonna to the Chiostro dei Morti (Cloister of the Dead) with its fresco of "Madonna del Sacco" (after the bag against which St Joseph is leaning), one of the major works of Andrea del Sarto (1525). Adjoining the Chiostro dei Morti are the chapter-house, the Cappella della Confraternità di San Luca, the "Chapel of the Crucified", the relic chapel and the sacristy.

The right-hand door leads to the Cappella Pucci or di San Sebastiano, and the two middle doors to the Chiostrino dei Voti ("Little Cloister of the Votive Offerings" after the votive offerings hung here by the faithful), the atrium built by Manetti (1447) to designs by Michelozzo.

Santissima Annunziata

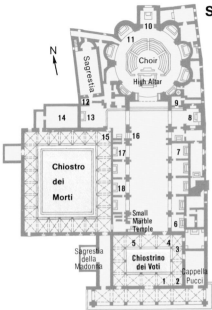

1 "Assunzione", by Rosso Fiorentino
2 "Visitazione", by Pontormo
3 "Natività di Maria", by Andrea del Sarto (1514)
4 "Arrivo dei Magi", by Andrea del Sarto (1511)
5 "Natività", by A. Baldovinetti (1460–62)
6 "Madonna in gloria, San Niccolò e Santi", by Empoli
7 Monument to Orlando de' Medici, by B. Rossellino
8 Cappella del Sacramento
9 Pietà, by B. Bandinelli (1559)
10 Cappella della Madonna del Soccorso, partly by Giambologna
11 "Resurrezione", by Bronzino, and wooden statue of St Roch, by Veit Stoss
12 Cappellina delle Reliquie
13 Cappella del Crocifisso
14 Cappella della Confraternità di San Luca
15 "Madonna del Sacco", by Andrea del Sarto
16 Organ dating from 1628
17 "Assunzione", by Perugino
18 "Santissima Trinità", fresco, by A. del Castagno (1454–5)

Chiostrino dei Voti

The early 16th c. frescoes in this atrium are famous. From left to right there are masterpieces by Andrea del Sarto (scenes from the life of St Filippo Benizzi); Cosimo Rosselli ("Vocation and Investiture of St Filippo Benizzi", 1476); Alesso Baldovinetto ("Nativity", 1460–2); another two by Andrea del Sarto ("Coming of the Magi" and, one of the artist's best works, "Birth of the Virgin", 1514) and Franciabigi's "Marriage of the Virgin", 1513, spoiled by the artist himself who destroyed Mary's head because the monks looked at the picture before its completion.

Finally there are more masterpieces by Pontormo ("Visitation of Mary", 1516) and Rosso Fiorentino ("Assumption of the Virgin", 1517).

Inside to the left of the entrance is a large marble tabernacle built at the behest of Piero de' Medici from a design by Michelozzo for the miraculous picture of the Annunciation of which there are many copies in Italy. It is said that the monk who was painting this picture in the 13th c. fell asleep out of despondency at his lack of skill when it came to depicting a wondrously fair Madonna and Mary's face was completed by an angel. Florentine newly-weds still come here and the bride leaves her bouquet by the Madonna.

Interior

The chapels are richly decorated with paintings and statues. The following are the most interesting (clockwise):

133

Left side
In the left aisle is the Cappella Feroni which contains a fresco by Andrea del Castagno, "Redeemer and St Julian" (1455).
The second chapel also has a fresco by Castagno, "Holy Trinity", one of his last highly realistic works. In the fourth chapel is a panel by Perugino, "Ascension of Christ".

Tribuna
Michelozzo began building the Tribuna, a rotunda divided into nine chapels, in 1451 and Leon Battista Alberti completed it to a different design. The fourth chapel from the left contains a painting by Angelo Bronzino, "Resurrection" (1550). The Cappella della Madonna del Soccorso (Madonna of Succour) was designed by Giambologna between 1594 and 1598 as his own tomb and is richly adorned with frescoes, statues and reliefs.

Dome
The dome is decorated with a fresco showing the Coronation of the Virgin by Volterrano (1681–3).

Right arm of the transept
Just inside the first chapel is a lovely "Pietà" by Baccio Bandinelli who is buried here with his wife.

** Santo Spirito (Church)   H6

Location
Piazza Santo Spirito

Buses
A, B

Several wealthy Florentine families joined forces in the early years of the 15th c. to build a new church on the site of one that had been burned down. They commissioned Brunelleschi, the city's famous architect, to design it. At the time of his death (1446) building work had progressed as far as the vaulting, but then it practically came to a standstill under various architects (bell-tower: Baccio d'Agnolo, 1503–17) and was never completed wholly in accordance with the original plans. This is why the austere exterior of the building shows no hint that Santo Spirito is one of the most purely Renaissance churches.
The façade of the church, which was consecrated in 1481, was executed in the 18th c. and is of bare plaster without ornamentation. It is characterized by its outline and the large round window in the middle. The façade has doors of different sizes corresponding to the nave and two aisles inside.

Interior

The interior is thought to be one of the most brilliant creations of the Florentine Renaissance. The plan is a Latin cross 318 ft (97 m) long, 108 ft (32 m) wide (transept 190 ft (58 m) wide) with a colonnaded central nave and side aisles and, built into the surrounding walls, forty semicircular side chapels. Its many works of art, tombs and monuments make Santo Spirito an impressive museum.
The side altars are resplendent with painting and statues, reliefs and liturgical objects. The visitor will find the following works of art of particular interest:

The rose-window in the façade was designed by Perugino ("Descent of the Holy Ghost"). The most important work in the church, "Madonna and Child with Saints and Donors", by Filippino Lippi (1490), is in the right arm of the transept, as is the marble sarcophagus of Neri di Gino Capponi, ascribed to

Santo Spirito

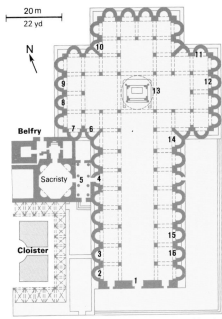

1 Window, "Discesa dello Spirito Santo", after Perugino
2 "Resurrezione", by di Jacopo
3 "Christo Risorto", by Landini, copy after Michelangelo
4 Access to the sacristy
5 Cronaca's vestibule, designed by G.da Sangallo
6 "Andata al Calvario", by M. Ghirlandaio
7 "Madonna col Bambino in trono e Santi", by dei Cari
8 "La Santissima Trinità adorata dalle Sante Caterina e Maddalena", by Granacci
9 Cappella Corbinelli, architecture and sculptures by Sansovino
10 "Presepio", by the school of Ghirlandaio
11 "Sposalizio della Vergine", by Sagrestani, and marble tomb of Neri di Gino Capponi
12 "Madonna col Bambino e San Giovannino", by F. Lippi
13 High altar by Caccini
14 "Raffaele e Tobiolo", marble panel, by Baratta (c. 1690)
15 San Nicola da Tolentino, wooden statue, by N. Unghero
16 Copy of Michelangelo's Pietà in Rome, by di Baccio Bigio (1549)

Bernardo Rossellino (1458). On the left-hand side of the apse there is an "Annunciation" (15th c. Florentine school) and a devout "Nativity" by the school of Ghirlandaio.

Sacristy
In the left-hand aisle is the entrance to a beautiful vestibule built by Cronaca (1492–4) with a door leading into the sacristy, an octagonal chamber designed by Giuliano da Sangallo (1495–6) and a masterpiece of European architecture.

Cloister
Another door in the vestibule leads into the first cloister, which is by Giulio and Alfonso Parigi (c. 1600). The second cloister, built by Ammanati between 1564 and 1569, is usually inaccessible because it is used for administrative purposes.

Left arm of the transept
It is worth having a look in the first chapel at Michele Ghirlandaio's painting, "Ascent of Calvary" and the glass in the window.
In the next chapel (moving clockwise) is Raffaele di Carli's panel, "Madonna in Majesty with Child" (1505).
In the second chapel along from this there is another panel, "Trinity worshipped by St Catherine and St Mary Magdalene", which is ascribed to Francesco Granacci.
Next door is the Cappella Corbinelli (sacramental chapel), exquisitely designed by Andrea Sansovino (1492), who was also responsible for the sculpture.

Cenacolo di Santo Spirito

Opening times
Tues.–Sat. 9 a.m.–2 p.m.;
Sun. and public holidays
8 a.m.–1 p.m.

Closed
Mon.

To the left of the church is the entrance to the Cenacolo di Santo Spirito. This refectory is all that remains of the old Augustinian monastery. It contains a large fresco of the Last Supper, attributed to Andrea Orcagna (c. 1360), which, though severely damaged, is one of the great 14th c. works of art in Florence. The refectory also houses the Salvatore Romano Foundation's fine sculptures.

*Santo Stefano al Ponte (Church)   J6

Location
Piazzeta Santo Stefano

In a small traffic-free square, mentioned in documents as early as 1116, is the church of Santo Stefano al Ponte (or "Santi Stefano e Cecilia"). The ravages of the Second World War and the 1966 floods have been righted and once again the church displays the elements of the various centuries (13th c. façade, 16th c. altars, 17th c. nave renovation) in all their glory.
The bronze relief, "The Stoning of St Stephen" is the work of Ferdinando Tocca (1656). Buontalenti's impressive marble staircase (1574) leading to the presbytery was formerly in the church of Santa Trinità (see entry).

Settignano

Location
5 miles (8 km) E

Bus
10

The Via Poggio to Settignano, a small town E of Florence, passes the villa where the company in Boccaccio's "Decamerone" sought refuge from the plague.
In San Martino a Mensola is the lovely church of the same name (with a triptych by Taddeo Gaddi) and not far from there is the villa known as "I Tatti", the headquarters, after the death in 1959 of the art critic Berenson, of Harvard University's Centre for Renaissance History. The "Collezione Berenson" contains valuable works of art.
Next comes the little Oratorio della Vannella, at Ponte a Mensola, and then Castello Vincigliata, the property of the Visdomini.
In Settignano it is worth paying a visit to the 15th c. parish church of the "Assunta", a building that has undergone several renovations. Nearby is the Villa Gamberaia, one of the finest villas of the 16th c. although damaged during the Second World War, where the gardens are extremely fine.

*Spedale degli Innocenti e Pinacoteca dello Spedale   K5
(Foundling Hospital and Art Gallery)

Location
Piazza della SS. Annunziata

Buses
1, 4 ,6, 7, 10, 11, 17, 25, 34

Times of opening
Mon., Tues., Thurs.–Sat.
9 a.m.–2 p.m.; Sun. and
public holidays 8 a.m.–1 p.m.

Closed
Wed.

In 1419 the guild of silk merchants and tailors commissioned the architect Filippo Brunelleschi, who built the dome of the cathedral (see Duomo Santa Maria del Fiore), to build a foundling hospital. Abandoned children were called Innocenti (Innocents) in remembrance of the children murdered in Bethlehem. Mothers who wanted to bring their new-born babies to the orphanage anonymously could (until 1875) place them in a revolving wooden cylinder ("Ruota") at the end of the portico. The Spedale degli Innocenti marks the beginning of Renaissance architecture in Florence.

Via Tornabuoni: one of the most interesting streets in the city

Garden and Villa Medicea di Castello

Loggia
The Spedale is famed for the harmonious colonnade of its
loggia. The consummate architecture is complemented by
frescoes under the arcades and in the lunettes above the doors,
as well as by the ten famous terracotta medallions by Andrea
della Robbia (c. 1463), each representing a baby in swaddling
clothes.

Santa Maria degli Innocenti
The porch leads to the church of Santa Maria degli
Innocenti with, beyond, a cloister designed by Brunelleschi
connected by a door with the church. In the lunette is a terracotta "Annunciation" by Andrea della Robbia.

Collection of frescoes
Besides the Pinacoteca dello Spedale degli Innocenti collection
there is also on the first floor a collection of detached frescoes
that have been removed from their original locations. They are
by Florentine artists including Poccetti, Bicci di Lorenzo,
Lorenzo Monaco, Allori, Rosselli, Ghirlandaio, Fra Bartolommeo, Perugino and della Robbia.

*Pinacoteca dello Spedale degli Innocenti (art gallery)

Opening times
Mon., Tues., Thurs.–Sat.
9 a.m.–2 p.m.; Sun. and
public holidays 8 a.m.–1 p.m.

Closed
Wed.

The Pinacoteca has a collection of pictures, sculptures,
miniatures and furniture dating from the 14th to the 18th c. Its
most notable exhibits include works by Giovanni del Biondo,
Rossellino and Benedetto da Maiano with those of Domenico
Ghirlandaio and Andrea del Sarto as well as Luca della
Robbia's terracotta "Madonna" meriting a special mention.

Uffizi

See Palazzo e Galleria degli Uffizi

Via Tornabuoni   J6

Location
between the Ponte
Santa Trinità and
the Piazza Antinori

One of the most elegant (because of its shops), most beautiful
(thanks to 19th c. planning) and most interesting (on account of
its 15th–19th c. palaces) streets in Florence, the Via Tornabuoni
is like a history book come to life, where the story of the city is
made manifest in splendid buildings: Palazzi Larderel-
Giacomini (early 16th c.), Corsi-Tornabuoni (1875, with a
courtyard by Michelozzo that survived from the Palazzo
Tornabuoni), Loggetta dei Tornaquinci (early 16th c.) and the
Palazzo Strozzi (17th c.).

Villa Romana   G8

Location
Via Senese 68

On the south side of the Arno, outside the medieval town walls,
Max Klinger acquired in 1905 the Villa Romana with the support
of the German Confederation of Artists. Its purpose was and is
to provide three (now four) artists with a place where they
could live and have a studio. In addition some of the rooms are
now used for temporary exhibitions.

Ville Medicee

The Medici family and its many relatives had at its disposal three villas to the NW of the city in the beautiful hills of Tuscany which they used as summer residences – the villas of Careggi, Petraia and Castello. Here the architects could give free rein to their skills and imagination – though within the framework of Renaissance architecture – as they worked on the buildings and gardens, while the artists, painters and sculptors were presented with plenty of opportunities to display the lighter side of their art.

Locations
Villa Medicea di Careggi:
Viale Pieraccini 17:
Villa Medicea della Petraia:
Via della Petraia a Castello:
Villa Medicea di Castello:
Via di Castello.

Practical Information A to Z

Airlines

Alitalia
Lungarno Acciaiuoli 10/12r, tel. 2 78 89
Flight Reservations, tel. 2 78 88

British Airways
Via della Vigna Nuova 36/38r, tel. 21 86 55

Pan Am
Lungarno Acciaiuoli 4, tel. 28 27 16

TWA
Piazza S. Trinità 2r, tel. 28 46 91

Airport

Florence airport, Peretola, is situated 3 miles/5 km north-west of the city (see Getting to Florence).

Banks, see Currency

Campsites (Campeggi)

In Italy campsites are, like hotels, designated by stars (1–5). The number of stars indicates the level of facilities, equipment and charges.

Florence

**Camping Michelangelo
Viale Michelangelo 80, tel. 6 81 19 77
Closed: Nov.–Mar.
380 pitches

*Villa di Camerata
Viale A. Righi 2/4; tel. 61 03 00
190 pitches

Barberino di Mugello

Campeggio Il Sergente
Via S. Lucia 24A Monte di Fò, tel. 8 42 30 18
80 pitches

Barberino Val d'Elsa

Campeggio Semifonte
Zona Sportiva, Bustecca, tel. 8 07 54 54
Closed: mid Oct.–Mar.
95 pitches

Calenzano

**Campeggio Autosole
Via Vittorio Emanuele II Spazzavento, tel. 88 23 91
70 pitches

***Campeggio Panoramico
Via Peramonda, tel. 59 90 69
190 pitches

Fiesole

***Campeggio Norcenni Girasole Club
Via di Norcenni 7, tel. 95 96 66
260 pitches

Figline Valdarno

**Camping Internaziole Firenze
Via San Cristofano 2 Bottai, tel. 2 02 04 45
Closed: Nov.–Mar.
240 pitches

Impruneta

***Campeggio Mugello Verde
La Fortezza, tel. 84 85 11
260 pitches

San Piero a Sieve

The Centro Internazionale Prenotazioni, Federcampeggio, Casella Postale 23, 50041 Calenzano (Firenze), tel. (055) 88 2391, can supply you with more information.

Car Rental (Autonoleggio)

Via Maso Finiguerra 33; tel. 28 22 60 and 29 82 05
(also at Peretola Airport and in the main rail station)

Hertz

Via L. Alamanni 7r; tel. 29 86 39 and 29 31 86
(also at Peretola Airport)

Avis

Via Borgo Ognissanti 113r; tel. 29 30 21 and 28 71 61

Budget

Via Borgo Ognissanti 53–59r; tel. 29 34 44 and 29 41 30
(also at Peretola Airport)

Europcar

Via Borgo Ognissanti 133r; tel 21 86 65 and 28 45 43
(also at Peretola Airport and in the main rail station)

InterRent

Via Maso Finiguerra 11r; tel. 21 02 38

Maggiore

Chemists (Farmacie)

Mon.–Fri. 8.30 a.m.–12.30 p.m. and 3.30–7.30 p.m.
(in summer 4–8 p.m.)

Opening times

Farmacia Comunale Nr. 13
in Santa Maria Novella station
tel. 26 34 35

Chemists open
throughout the day

Farmacia Molteni
Via Calzaiuoli 7r
tel. 26 34 90

Farmacia Taverna
Piazza San Giovanni 20r
tel. 28 40 13

Practical Information

Night service

In every district of the city there is a chemist open day and night. The chemist on duty can be found in the daily newspapers or by telephoning 192.

Consulates

United Kingdom

Palazzo Castelbarco Lungarno Corsini 2,
tel. 28 41 33

United States

Lungarno Amerigo Vespucci 38,
tel. 29 82 76

Currency

Currency

The unit of currency is the *lira* (plural *lire*).
There are banknotes for 1000, 2000, 5000, 10,000, 20,000, 50,000 and 100,000 lire and coins in denominations of 5, 10, 20, 50, 100, 200 and 500 lire.

Lira Nuova

The Italian parliament has been discussing currency reform for years. It is proposed to introduce a "new lira" which will be worth 1000 old lire. If and when the necessary legislation will be introduced remains uncertain. When the change takes place the old lira will remain in circulation with the new for two years.

Import of currency

There are no restrictions on the import of currency into Italy, but in view of the strict control on the export of currency it is advisable to declare any currency brought in on the appropriate form (*modulo V2*) at the frontier.

Export of currency

The export of foreign currency is permitted only up to a value of 5,000,000 lire per person except where a larger sum has been declared on entry. No more than 1,000,000 lire of Italian currency can be taken out.

Eurocheques

Eurocheques can be used up to a value of 300,000 lire.

Credit cards

Banks, the larger hotels and restaurants, car rental firms and many shops accept the principal international credit cards. The most widely used in Italy is Visa, followed by American Express, Eurocard/Access and Diners Club.

Banks, Currency Exchange

Opening times for banks: Mon.–Fri. 8.30 a.m.–1.30 or 2.30 p.m. Some banks are open for an hour in the afternoon, usually 3–4 p.m.
Outside normal opening times money can be exchanged at Santa Maria Novella Rail Station (Eurocheques not accepted). Opening times are: in summer Mon.–Sat. 8.20 a.m.–1.20 p.m. and 2.45–4 p.m.

Postcheques

Postcheques, up to a maximum value of 3,000,000 lire per cheque, may be cashed at post offices (posta) where you see the "Postcheque" sign. (See "Postal services" for opening hours).

Customs regulations

Visitors to Italy from the European Community can take in, without payment of duty, articles for their personal use; in addition persons over 15 can take in 1000 grams of coffee or 400 grams of powdered coffee, and 200 grams of tea or 80 grams of tea extract. Visitors over 17 can import 1 litre of spirits above 22° or 2 litres of spirits below 22°, or 2 litres of still table wine (in which case the 1 litre spirit allocation is in addition to the wine); 50 grams of perfume and 250 cc of toilet water; also 200 cigarettes, 100 cigarillos or 50 cigars or 250 grams of tobacco. Persons over 15 can also bring in goods and gifts to an equivalent value of £32.
The duty-free allowance for those living *outside Europe* is the same except for the tobacco allowance which is double the limits indicated.
For goods obtained *duty and tax-paid* in the European Community, import allowances are increased.
Importing weapons, whether real or imitation, sheath and combination knives is prohibited. Fuel in canisters may not be imported. If on entry into Italy a visitor has fairly large sums of cash, it is advisable fore this to be declared (see Currency).

Visitors can take out, without liability to duty, articles which they have bought in Italy up to a value of 520,000 lire. For the export of objets d'art and antiques a permit must be obtained from the Italian Ministry of Education (Export Department).

Entry (margin)

Departures (margin)

Events

Florence Trade Fair (leather goods and clothes)	January
Aureo Trade (Fair of goldsmiths' work)	February
Furniture Fair	March
Easter Sunday; Scoppio del Carro ("burning of a cart" between cathedral and baptistery)	March/April
International Handicraft Fair (until May) Easter Sunday: Scoppio del Carro (firework display in the Cathedral Square)	April
Ascension Day: Spring festival ("Festa del grillo") in the Parco delle Cascine Maggio Musicale Fiorentino: Music festival with international artistes (until June)	May
24 June: Festival of St John the Baptist (patron saint of Florence) and fireworks Firenze estate (Florentine summer): cultural and musical events (until September) Calcio Storico Fiorentino, revival of the football match in medieval costumes (3 matches) Palio Remiero: rowing contests on the Arno	June
Horse racing	July

143

Practical Information

August	Pitti Bimbo (Fair of children's fashions) International leather goods fair
September	Pitti Uomo (Fair of men's fashions) Pitti Filate (Fair of knitwear, etc.) Casual (Fair of leisurewear fashions) Festa delle rificolone (feast of lanterns; 7 September) Oltarno di Firenze (September festival) Horse racing (also in October and November)
October	Antiques Fair Pitti Donna (Fair of women's fashions) Exhibition of plants and flowers
November	Start of the opera, concert and theater season Italian ophthalmic exhibition
December	Christmas cribs (Nativity groups) in numerous locations

Excursions (Escursioni)

Bus tours	Excursions in the immediate vicinity of Florence (multi-ligual guides) can be booked at most travel agents and also at the national C.I.T. (Compagnia Italiana Turismo). Tourist Office (Via Cavour 54r; tel.29 43 06 and Piazza Stazione 51r; tel. 28 41 45). From April to June the "Agriturist" organisation runs excursions visiting the gardens of the most beautiful villas of Florence. Departures Tues., Thurs., and Sat. 2.15 p.m. from the Piazza Santa Maria Novella. Booking can be made at travel agents or direct from Agriturist (Piazza San Firenze 3; tel. 28 78 38). There are excursions visiting farms and estates around Florence in September and October.
Fiesole, Certosa del Galluzzo	In the immediate vicinity of Florence the little town of Fiesole and the Certosa del Galluzzo, Carthusian monastery (see entries A to Z), are well worth seeing.
Barberino Val D'Elsa	On the old Roman road, 22 miles/35 km south of Florence, is Barberino Val d'Elsa. Its defensive walls served the citizens of Florence in their war against Siena. The Porta Senese, the only gate in the ring of walls, dates from the 14th c. The Palazzo Pretorio and the parish church of San Bartolomeo are also worth seeing.
Certaldo	Certaldo, 19 miles/30 km south-west of Florence, boasts some well preserved medieval houses and palaces.
Castelfiorentino	Castelfiorentino is situated 25 miles/40 km south-west of Florence in the valley of the river Elsa. The town, founded as a bastion against the Sienese, has two attractive churches and a small picture gallery.
Empoli, Vinci	22 miles/35 km along the Pisa road lies the modern industrial town of Empoli. Of interest are the collegiate Church of St Andrew, the Church of Santo Stefano and the collegiate museum. Some 6 miles/10 km north of Empoli is Vinci, the birthplace of the brilliant artist Leonardo da Vinci (museum and house where he was born).

Borgo San Lorenzo, 19 miles/30 km north of Florence is worth visiting to see the church dedicated to St Laurence, the patron saint of the town.
The chief features of Scarperia, 6 miles/10 km north-west of Borgo San Lorenzo, are the Palazzo Pretorio and the Protestant church.

Borgo San Lorenzo, Scarperia

First aid (Pronto Soccorso)

Tel. 113 (applies throughout Italy)

Emergencies

Croce Rossa Italiana (Red Cross)
Lungarno Soderini 11; tel. 21 53 81

Medical help

Pubblica Assistenza Humanitas
Via Paisiello 18; tel. 35 65 35

Sundays and public holidays, tel. 47 54 11

Doctor on call

Tel. 21 22 22

Accident assistance

Food and drink

Although most hotels now serve a full continental breakfast, the Italians themselves are content with a quick espresso coffee in a bar and perhaps a cornetto (roll). At midday and in the evening substantial meals are taken. A typical lunch or dinner consists of a cold or hot starter ("antipasto"), the next course ("primo") with noodles ("pasta"), followed by a main dish ("secundo") of meat or fish, and then cheese ("formaggio") and a dessert ("dolce").
Lunch ("pranzo" or "colazione") is usually taken between 1 and 3 p.m. and dinner between 7 and 10 p.m.

Meals

Gastronomically Italy is second only to France among the countries of Europe. In contrast to France, Italy places less emphasis on presentation and refinement. Particularly in Tuscany the cuisine has until now retained its simple country style, which is distinguished by the purity and quality of the ingredients and by careful preparation according to simple traditional recipes. Less attention is given to pasta dishes than in the rest of Italy; instead of this the starter often consists of many kinds of unsalted home-made bread often accompanied by soup. Meat and fish are usually baked or fried in Tuscan olive oil which is often added to tasty stews. Important ingredients of a meal are a rich variety of vegetables and especially aromatic herbs.

Italian/Tuscan cuisine

Although soups are generally served in other parts of Italy before the main course, in Tuscany they are often consummed before the "antipasta".
Almost everywhere in Italy the menu will feature a "minestrone". This includes white beans, celery, onions, peas, ham, tomato purée, garlic and a little wine. Typical Tuscan soups are "zuppa di pane", a cabbage soup with bread and additional vegetables, "ribollita", the most important ingredients of

Soups

145

which are white beans, olive oil, bread and cheese. It tastes better when it is hot. For "zuppa di fagioli alla fiorentina" white beans are braised in olive oil and cooked with onions, garlic, cabbage, leeks, bread and herbs.

Starters

Noodles, of course, are not absent from Tuscan cuisine. "Cannelloni ripeni alla toscana" consists of pasta filled with a mixture of meat, chicken liver, truffles, eggs and Parmesan cheese; "agnolotti alla toscana" is ravioli filled with meat, spinach, Parmesan cheese and spices. "Pappardelle alla lepre" is made from egg noodles and stewed hare.

If you do not like noodles you could try "tortino di carciofi", baked artichokes with beaten egg and herbs, or "crostini di fegatini", a chicken liver pâté with capers and sardines served on white bread.

Fish dishes

Tuscan cuisine also has speciality fish dishes including "baccalà alla livornese" consisting of boiled dried cod filled with tomatoes. To prepare "triglie all livornese" fresh sea barbel are cooked with a light sauce of tomatoes and refined oil. Not specifically Tuscan but featured on almost every menu are "calamari fritti", fried rings of squid or "orate ai ferri", baked red mullet.

Meat dishes

The best known Tuscan meat dish is certainly "bistecca alla fiorentina", a T-bone steak cooked on a charcoal grill without added fat and then sprinkled with olive oil. Tuscan dishes are typically prepared with a mixture of herbs, wild berries, garlic, oil, wine and vinegar; among these are: "arista alla fiorentina", loin of pork spiced with rosemary and cloves or "pollo alla diavola", chicken flavoured with sage and cooked on a charcoal grill. Another speciality of Tuscan cuisine is offal, such as "trippa alla fiorentine", which is cooked in a sauce of tomatoes and Parmesan cheese, and "fegatini di maiale", laurel leaves stuffed with pigs liver and cooked on a spit.

Deserts

The best sweets in Italy have been produced in Tuscany for centuries. "Panforte di Siena", a kind of gingerbread made from almonds, candied fruits, flour, butter and eggs is exported all over the world.

Florence is well known for its "zuccotto", a soft ice desert made from biscuit crust, chocolate cream, with a cream filling. Very tempting are "castagnaccio", a cake of chestnut purée with pine kernels and candied fruits, and "schiacciata alla fiorentina", a cake made from flour, olive oil, eggs and lard; if the cook adds red grapes it is called "schiacciata con l'uva".

Drinks

Generally wine (see entry) and water are drunk with meals; beer is obtainable everywhere but in comparison with wine is often considerably more expensive.

The Italians nearly always finish a meal with coffee. A small dark strong coffee which, outside Italy, is often known as an espresso, is called in Italy simply "caffè" and served either "doppio" (large), "corretto" with grappa, cognac or bitters added, "freddo" (cold) or "ristretto" (weak). Another variant is "cappuccino" (topped with foaming milk); it can be ordered "chiaro" (light) or "scuro" (dark), at various temperatures and with more or less milk foam. A simple coffee with milk is a "caffelatte" or "macchiato"; if milk with a little coffee is preferred then a "latte macchiato" should be ordered.

Galleries (Gallerie)

Collezione Contini-Bonacossi
See Museums

Galleria dell'Accademia (Art Museum of the Academy)
See A–Z

Galleria d'Arte Moderna (Gallery of Modern Art)
See A–Z, Palazzo Pitti

Galleria Rinaldo Carnielo (Sculpture)
Piazza Savonarola 18
Open: Sat. 9 a.m.–1 p.m. Admission free.

Galleria Corsini
See A–Z, Palazzo Corsini

Galleria del Costume (Costume Gallery)
See A–Z, Palazzo Pitti

Galleria Ferroni
See A–Z

Galleria Palatina/Galleria Pitti
See A–Z, Palazzo Pitti

Galleria Strozzina
See A–Z, Palazzo Strozzi

Galleria degli Uffizi
See A–Z, Palazzo degli Uffizi

Pinacoteca dello Spedale degli Innocenti
See A–Z, Spedale degli Innocenti

Raccolta di Arte Moderna "A. della Ragione"
Piazza Signoria 5
Open: Mon., Wed.–Sat. 9 a.m.–2 p.m.; Sun. 8 a.m.–1 p.m.
Closed: Tues.

Centro Tornabuoni (international modern art)   Art Sales
Via Tornabuoni 5

Galleria Bellini (antiques)
Lungarno Soderini 5

Mirteto (modern art)
Via Maggio 7

Galleria Orlando (modern art)
Via Giglio 12r

Galleria San Marco (water colours and oil paintings)
Via Ricasoli 95r

See entry   Museums

Gasoline (petrol or "benzina")

In Italy the cost of motor fuel (apart from diesel) is considerably
above the European average. Tourists taking their car to Italy
are entitled to a reduction on the normal price of petrol

supergrade only), they are issued with gasoline (petrol) coupons, generally as a "packet" with coupons for the Italian superhighways (motorways), for the use of which tolls are charged. The packet must be purchased outside of Italy or from the Automobile Club d'Italia (ACI) at principal Italian frontier points. Information can be obtained from the motoring organisations' appointed agents and the ENIT (Italian State Tourist Office).

Lead-free fuel

The availability of lead-free motor fuel in northern Italy is relatively good, especially on motorways. A list of gasoline stations supplying lead-free fuel can be obtained from motoring organisations. However, as you can never be completely certain that every filling station has supplies, you are advised to fill up as often as possible. Pumps dispensing unleaded fuel are marked in English "Super Unleaded".

Spare fuel

For reasons of safety the carrying of cans of fuel in vehicles is prohibited in Italy.

Credit cards

These are rarely accepted at petrol stations.

Getting to Florence

By car

It is a long way from Britain or northern Europe to Florence. Motorists will be well advised, therefore, to use superhighways (motorways) and main trunk roads as far as possible.

Highways

Tolls are payable on most Italian highways (autostrade). The tickets for each section should be retained, since they must be given up when leaving the highway, when payment is usually made.

Documents, etc.

The minimum age which a visitor may use a temporarily imported car is 18 years. Motorists should carry their driving licence and car registration document. A translation of the licence, obtainable from motoring clubs or the ENIT (Italian State Tourist Office), is normally required but not for the "pink" EC type licence. An international insurance certificate ("green card") is not obligatory but is advisable (see Insurance). The car should have a nationality plate, and a warning triangle must be carried.

Roads to Florence

Although there are several ways of getting to Italy, entry will most probably be by way of France or Switzerland. The major passes, which are closed in winter, are served by road or rail tunnels. The distance to Florence from the Channel ports is approximately 850–890 miles (1370–1430 km), requiring one or two night stops. Car-sleeper services operate during the summer from Boulogne, Brussels or Paris to Milan and Boulogne to Bologna.

Frontier crossings

France–Italy, open 24 hours. Mont Blanc Tunnel: Chamonix–Aosta; Fréjus Tunnel: Chambéry–Turin.
Switzerland–Italy. The major frontier crossings between Switzerland and Italy, open 24 hours a day, are:
St Bernard (road tunnel): Lausanne–Aosta (the pass is usually closed from October to June); Simplon Pass (the pass is

occasionally closed during the winter; alternative rail tunnel available): Brig–(rail tunnel NOT 24 hour service) Milan; Chiasso: Lugano–Como–Milan; Castasegna/Chiavenna (Maloja Pass): St Moritz–Milan.

Austria–Italy. The following frontier crossings between Austria and Italy are open 24 hours a day:

Brenner Pass: Innsbruck–Bolzano; Résia (Reschen) Pass: Landeck–Merano–Bolzano; Arnbach/Prato alla Drave: Lienz–Dobbiaco–Cortina; Tarvisio: Villach–Udine–Venice.

There are numerous package tours by bus, either going direct to Florence or including Florence in a longer circuit. For information apply to any travel agent.
There are also various scheduled bus services between Britain or northern Europe and Florence.

By bus

The only services to Florence airport from abroad are run from Munich and Nuremberg. There are scheduled flights from London to Milan and Pisa and a weekly service from Manchester to Milan. From these airports Florence can be reached by train or bus. Trains from Pisa (Galileo Galilei) airport, connect with international flights for the one hour journey between the airport terminal and Florence.

By air

The fastest route from London to Florence takes just about 17 hours, leaving London (Victoria) at 10 a.m., crossing the Channel by hovercraft and changing in Paris. An alternative route, via Hook of Holland to Florence, leaves London (Liverpool Street at 9.45 a.m. (9.20 a.m. Sun.), changing at Cologne and arriving at Florence at 15.20 on the next day.

By rail

See Rail services, p. 163.

Rail services

Hospitals (Ospedali)

Generale di Careggi
Viale Morgagni; tel. 4 39 91

Ospedale Nuovo di San Giovanni di Dio
Via Torregalli 3; tel. 2 76 61

Ospedale di Santa Maria Nuovo
Palazzo Santa Maria Nuovo; tel. 2 75 81

Pediatrico Meyer (children's hospital)
Via Luca Giordano 14; tel. 4 39 91

Istituto Ortopedico Toscana "Piero Palagi" (orthopaedic clinic)
Viale Michelangelo 41; tel. 2 76 91

Ospedale Oftalmico Fiorentino (eye clinic)
Via Masaccio 213; tel. 57 84 44

Practical Information

Hotels (Alberghi)

Categories

Hotels are officially classified in five categories, from deluxe hotel (5 stars) to hotel or guesthouse with modest facilities (one star).
The following hotel list is arranged according to this classification. The address and telephone number are followed by the number of beds; "SP" designates a hotel with a pool.

Tariffs

Tariffs vary considerably according to season. The rates given in the following table (in lire) are based on information given in the Italian State Tourist Office's list of hotels (1988). "Alberghi d'Italia". Increases are to be expected. Service charges are included in rates, and VAT (IVA in Italy) at 10 per cent (18 per cent in deluxe class) also operates. Hotel bills should be kept in case of enquiry by government inspectors into possible tax evasion.

Category	Single room Rate for 1 person	Double room Rate for 2 persons
*****	180,000–370,000	250,000–550,000
****	80,000–180,000	110,000–240,000
***	45,000–70,000	60,000–105,000
**	35,000–45,000	50,000–60,000
*	25,000–30,000	35,000–45,000

*****

Excelsior, Piazza Ognissanti 3, tel. 26 42 01, 377 b.
Grand Hotel, Piazza Ognissanti, tel. 27 87 81, 70 b.
Grand Hotel Villa Cora, Viale Machiavelli 18, tel. 2 29 84 51, 97 b., SP
Regency Umbria, Piazza M. D'Azeglio 3, tel. 24 52 47, 50 b.
Savoy, Piazza della Repubblica 7, tel. 28 33 13, 180 b.
Villa Medici, Via il Prato 42, tel. 26 13 31, 198 b., SP

****

Alexander, Viale Giudoni 101, tel. 4 37 89 51, 168 b.
Anglo-American, Via Garibaldi 9, tel. 28 21 14, 202 b.
Astoria Pullman, Via Del Giglio 9, tel. 29 80 95, 163 b.
Atlantic Palace, Via Nationale 12, tel. 21 30 31, 86 b.
Augustus & Dei Congressi, Vicolo dell'Oro 5, tel. 28 30 54, 129 b.
Crest Hotel, Viale Europa 205, tel. 68 68 41, 84 b., SP
Croce di Malta, Via della Scala 7, tel. 28 26 00, 184 b., SP
De la Ville, Piazza Antinori 1, tel. 26 18 06, 135 b.
Fenice Palace, Via Martelli 10, tel. 26 39 42, 114 b.
Grand Hotel Baglioni, Piazza Unità Italiana 6, tel. 21 84 41, 359 b.
Grand Hotel Majestic, Via del Melarancio 1, tel. 26 40 21, 185 b.
Grand Hotel Minerva, Piazza Santa Maria Novella 16, tel. 28 45 55, 198 b., SP
Jolly Carlton, Piazza V. Veneto 4A, tel. 27 70, 293 b., SP
Kraft, Via Solferino 2, tel. 28 42 73, 120 b., SP
Londra, Via Jacopo da Diacceto 18/20, tel. 26 27 91, 178 b.
Lungarno, Borgo San Jacopo 14, tel. 26 42 11, 101 b.
Michelangelo, Viale Fratelli Rosselli 2, tel. 27 87 11, 253 b.
Milano Terminus, Via Cerretani 10, tel. 28 33 72, 136 b.
Monginevro, Via di Novoli 59, tel. 43 14 41, 220 b.
Montebello Splendid, Via Montebello 60, tel. 29 80 51, 73 b.
Park Palace, Piazzale Galileo 5, tel. 22 24 31, 52 b., SP
Pierre, Via Lamberti 5, tel. 21 62 18, 78 b.

Principe, Lungarno Vespucci 34, tel. 28 48 48, 35 b.
Raffaello, Viale Morgagni 19, tel. 43 98 71, 276 b.
Ritz, Lungarno Zecca Vecchia 24, tel. 2 34 06 50, 50 b.
Villa Belvedere, Via Castelli 3, tel. 22 25 01, 51 b., SP
Villa Carlotta, Via Michele di Lando 3, tel. 22 05 30, 46 b.

Adriatico, Via Maso Finiguerra 9, tel. 26 17 81, 222 b.   ***
Ambasciatori, Via Alamanni 3, tel. 28 74 21, 165 b.
Aprile, Via della Scala 6, tel. 21 62 37, 48 b.
Auto Park Hotel, Via Valdegola 1, tel. 43 17 71, 198 b.
Balestri, Piazza Mentana 7, tel. 21 47 43, 87 b.
Bonciani, Via Panzani 17, tel. 26 23 41, 106 b.
Capitol, Viale Amendola 34, tel. 23 43 201, 141 b.
Cavour, Via del Pronconsolo 3, tel. 28 71 02, 116 b.
Columbus, Lungarno C. Colombo 22A, tel. 67 72 51, 156 b.
Concorde, Viale Luigi Gori 10, tel. 37 35 51, 146 b.
Corona, Via Nazionale 14, tel. 27 86 31, 143 b.
Duomo, Piazza Duomo 1, tel. 21 99 22, 46 b.
Firenze Nova, Via Panciatichi 51, tel. 47 78 51, 246 b.
Fleming, Viale Guidoni 87, tel. 43 76 331, 174 b.
Golf, Viale Fratelli Rosselli 56, tel. 29 30 88, 70 b.
Helvetia E Bristol, Via dei Pescioni 2, tel. 28 78 14, 101 b.
Mediterraneo, Lungarno del Tempio 44, tel. 66 02 41, 668 b.
Porta Rossa, Via Porta Rossa 19, tel. 28 75 51, 130 b.
Royal, Via delle Ruote 52, tel. 48 32 87, 50 b.
San Remo, Lungarno Serristori 13, tel. 23 42 823, 35 b.
Villa Le Rondini, Via Bolognese Vecchia 224, tel. 40 00 81, 51 b.,
SP

Alessandra, Borgo SS Apostoli 17, tel. 28 34 38, 44 b.   **
Arno Bellariva, Lungarno del Tempio 16, tel. 66 63 42, 41 b.
Autostrada, Viale L. Gori 31, tel. 37 18 56, 86 b., SP
Bellettini, Via dei Conti 7, tel. 21 35 61, 40 b.
Capri, Via XXVII Aprile 3, tel. 21 54 41, 94 b.
Careggi, Via T. Alderotti 43, tel. 43 60 262, 50 b.
Delle Nazioni, Via Alamanni 15, tel. 28 35 75, 155 b.
La Terrazza, Via Taddea 8, tel. 29 43 22, 48 b.
Nuovo Atlantico, Via Nazionale 10, tel. 21 66 22, 174 b.
Splendor, Via San Gallo 30, tel. 48 34 27, 52 b.

Casci, Via Cavour 13, tel. 21 16 86, 40 b.   *
Firenze, Piazza Donati 4, tel. 21 42 03, 84 b.
Il Perseo, Via Cerretani 1, tel. 21 25 04, 46 b.
Imperia, Via Rosina 7, tel. 28 71 41, 51 b.
La Romagnola, Via della Scala 40, tel. 21 15 97, 47 b.
Residenza Universitaria Fiorentina, Viale Don Minzoni 25,
tel. 57 65 52, 108 b.
Universo, Piazza Santa Maria Novella 20, tel. 21 14 84, 68 b.
Villa Natalia, Via Bolognese 106, tel. 49 07 73, 44 b.

Consorzio Informazioni Turistiche Alberghiere (I.T.A.)   Hotel Reservations
In Santa Maria Novella Station, tel 28 28 93
Open: 9 a.m.–8.30 p.m.

Cooperative Alberghiere
(reservations only for hotels in the group)
Coopal
Via il Prato 2r, tel. 21 95 25/29 21 92

Florence Promhotels
Viale Volta 72, tel. 57 04 81

Practical Information

Hotel Agent
Piazza Pier Vettori 10, tel. 22 36 67

Toscana Hotels
Viale Gramsci 9A, tel. 2 47 85 43–5

C.R.A.T. Consorzio Regionale Aziende Turistiche della
Toscana, c/o A.T.A.V.
Via Martelli 5, tel. 29 49 00
(reservations by mail only)

Albergo Diurno
(day hotel)

Diurno Stazione Santa Maria Novella
Piazza S.M. Novella, tel. 21 52 88

In this hotel rooms can be rented by the hour in order to wash take a bath or get a shave and a haircut.

Insurance

Car insurance

It is very desirable to have an international insurance certificate ("Green card"), although this is not a legal requirement for citizens of EC countries. It is important to have fully comprehensive cover, and it is desirable to take out short-term insurance against legal costs if these are not already covered. Italian insurance companies tend to be slow in settling claims.

Health insurance

British visitors to Italy, like other EC citizens, are entitled to receive health care on the same basis as Italians (including free medical treatment, etc.); they should apply to their local Departments of Health, well before their date of departure, for a certificate of entitlement (form E111). Fuller cover can be obtained for the duration of your stay by taking out insurance against medical expenses for those in private patients schemes (e.g. BUPA); and non-EC citizens will, of course, be well advised to take out appropriate insurance cover.

Baggage insurance

In view of the risk of theft it is desirable to have adequate insurance against loss of, or damage to, baggage.

Language

Language

The Italian language is a direct descendant of Latin, to which it is closer than any other of the Romance languages. Numerous dialects developed, largely in consequence of the earlier political fragmentation of Italy, and among these Tuscan became accepted as the standard language, created by the great writers of the 13th and 14th c., paricularly Dante. The language of the educated Florentine is considered as the purest form of Italian.

In the larger hotels and restaurants of Florence English is understood and spoken by many of the staff. Nevertheless a few Italian words and expressions will often be useful.

Pronunciation

The stress is usually on the second last syllable. Where it falls on the last syllable this is always indicated by an accent (perché, cittá). Where the stress is on the last syllable but two an accent is not officially required, except in certain doubtful cases, but it is sometimes shown as an aid to pronunciation.

Consonants: c before e or i is pronounced ch, otherwise like k; g before e or i is pronounced like j, otherwise hard (as in "go"); gn and gl are like n and l followed by a consonantal y (roughly as in "onion" and "million"). h is silent, qu as in English; r is rolled; s is unvoiced (as in "so") at the beginning of a word before a vowel, but has the sound of z between vowels and before b, d, g, l, m, n and vv; sc before e or i is pronounced sh, z is either like ts or ds. Vowels are pronounced in the "continental" fashion, without the diphthongisation normal in English; e is never silent. The vowels in a diphthong are pronounced separately (ca-usa, se-i).

0	zero	12	dodici	Numbers
1	uno, una, un, un'	13	tredici	
2	due	14	quattordici	
3	tre	15	quindici	
4	quattro	16	sedici	
5	cinque	17	diciasette	
6	sei	18	diciotto	
7	sette	19	deciannove	
8	otto	20	venti	
9	nove	21	ventuno	
10	dieci	22	ventidue	
11	undici	30	trenta	

31	trentuno	100	cento
40	quaranta	101	cento uno
50	cinqanta	153	centocinquantatre
60	sessanta	200	duecento
70	settanta	1000	mile
80	ottanta	5000	cinque mila
90	novanta	1 million	un milione

1st	primo (prima)	7th	settimo	Ordinals
2nd	secundo	8th	ottavo	
3rd	terzo	9th	nono	
4th	quarto	10th	decimo	
5th	quinto	20th	ventesimo/vigesimo	
6th	sesto	100th	centesimo	

½	un mezzo (mezza)	Fractions
¼	un quarto	
¹⁄₁₀	un decimo	

Good morning, good day!	Boun giorno!	Everyday expressions
Good evening!	Buona sera!	
Goodbye	Arrivaderci!	
Yes, no	Si, no!	
I beg your pardon	Scusi	
Please	Per favore	
Thank you (very much)	(Molte) gracie!	
Not at all (you're welcome)	Prego	
Excuse me (when passing in front of someone)	Con permesso	
Do you speak English?	Parla inglese	
A little, not much	Un poco, non molto	
I do not understand	Non capisco	
What is the Italian for . . .	Come si dice . . . in italiano?	

What is the name of this church?	Come si chiama questa chiesa
The cathedral	Il duomo
The square	La piazza
The palace	Il palazzo
The theatre	Il teatro
Where is the Via . . . ?	Dov'è la via X?
Where is the road (motorway) to . . . ?	Dov'è la strada (l'autostrada) per . . . ?
Left, right	A sinistra, a destra
Straight ahead	Sempre diretto
Above, below	sopra, sotto
When is (it) open?	Quando è aperto?
How far is it?	Quando è distante?
Today	Oggi
Yesterday	Ieri
The day before yesterday	L'altro ieri
Tomorrow	Domani
Have you any rooms?	Ci sono camere libere?
I should like	Vorrei avere . . .
A room with bath (shower)	Una camera con bagno (doccia)
With full board	Con pensione completa
What does it cost?	Qual'è il prezzo? Quanto costa?
All-in (price)	Totto compreso
That is too dear	E troppo caro
Bill, please (to a waiter)	Cameriere, il conto!
Where are the lavatories?	Dove si trovano i gabinetti? (il servizi, la ritrata)
Wake me at six	Può sveliami alle sei!
Where is there a doctor (dentist)?	Dove sta un mèdico (un dentista)?

At the post office	Address	Indirezzo
	Airmail	Posta aerea
	Express	Espresso
	Letter	Léttera
	Post box	Buca delle lettere
	Postcard	Cartolina
	Poste restante	Fermo posta
	Postman	Postino
	Stamp	Francobollo
	Registered letter	Léttera raccomandata
	Telegram	Telegramma
	Telephone	Telefono
Travelling	Aircraft	Aeroplano
	Airport	Aeroporto
	Arrival	Arrivo
	Baggage (luggage)	Bagagli
	Booking office	Sportello
	Bus (tram) stop	Fermata
	Change (trains)	Cambiare treno
	Departure (air)	Partenza (Decollo)
	Departure (rail)	Partenza
	Fare	Prezzo di biglietto, (Tariffa)
	Flight	Volo

No smoking	Vietato fumare	
Guard	Capotreno	
Platform	Marciapiede	
Porter	Portabaglagli, (faccino)	
Station	Stazione	
Stop	Sosta	
Ticket collector	Conduttore	
Timetable	Orario	
Track	Binario	
Waiting room	Sala d'asspetto	
Monday	Lunedi	Weekdays
Tuesday	Martedi	
Wednesday	Mercoledi	
Thursday	Giovedi	
Friday	Venerdi	
Saturday	Sabato	
Sunday	Domenica	
Day	Giorno	
Weekday	Giorno feriale	
Holiday	Giorno festivo	
Week	Settimana	
New year	Capo d'anno	Holidays
Easter	Pasqua	
Whitsun	Pentecoste	
Christmas	Natale	
January	Gennaio	Months
February	Febbraio	
March	Marzo	
April	Aprile	
May	Maggio	
June	Giugno	
July	Luglio	
August	Agosto	
September	Settembre	
October	Ottobre	
November	Novembre	
December	Dicembre	

Lost property offices (Servizi oggetti rinvenuti)

Ufficio Oggetti smarriti
Via Circondaria 19, tel. 36 79 43

Municipal lost property office

Ufficio Oggetti rinvenuti
Santa Maria Novella Railroad Station
Central office, tel. 27 67

Railroad lost property office

Markets (Mercati)

Mercato del Piccolo Antiquariato
Piazza del Ciompi (open daily)

Flea Market
Antiques

Fruit and vegetable markets – part of daily life

Weekly market	Mercato delle Cascine Parco delle Cascine (clothing, etc.; open on Tuesdays)
Provisions	Mercato Centrale Piazza del Mercato Centrale; near San Lorenzo Open in the mornings
	Mercato Sant'Ambrogio Piazza Ghiberti (fruit, vegetables, meat, cheese) Open in the mornings
Leather/ souvenirs	Loggia di Mercato Nuovo Piazza del Porcellino (also craftwork in straw, ceramics and knitwear)
	Loggia degli Uffizi Piazzale degli Uffizi (open daily)

Motoring

In general traffic regulations in Italy do not differ essentially from those in other European countries where vehicles travel on the right. Traffic signs are those internationally agreed.

The inner city of Florence (blue zone or "zona disco") is barred to private cars on Mon.–Sat. from 8 a.m. to 6 p.m. This may not be immediately apparent to visitors, as there are many exceptions. Tourists may use their cars in the blue zone for loading and unloading luggage, but must then remove their vehicle to a hotel car park or to a car park outside the restricted zone. Discs, which are displayed on car windscreens and allow parking for a restricted time, are obtainable from petrol stations and motoring organisations.

Blue zone

Within built-up areas the speed limit is 31 m.p.h. (50 km p.h.); outside these areas new regulations came into force in 1988. From Monday to Friday private cars can travel on the motorways at speeds up to 81 m.p.h. (130 km p.h.). On Saturdays and Sundays, and on public holidays and the day preceding them, the limit is 68 m.p.h. (110 km p.h.). This lower limit also applies to holiday times, when traffic is heavy and vehicles up to 1099cc. The speed limit for cars on main roads is 56 m.p.h. (90 km p.h.). Cars towing trailers or caravans are limited to 62 m.p.h. (100 km p.h.) on motorways; 49 m.p.h. (80 km p.h.) on main roads; and 31 m.p.h. (50 km p.h.) in built-up areas.

Speed limits

Speed limits for motorcyclists depend on the size of the engine. Up to 99 cc it is 51 m.p.h. (80 km p.h.) on main roads; up to 149 cc the limit on main roads is 56 m.p.h. (90 km p.h.). Motorcycles with engine exceeding 150 cc are subject to the same speed limits as cars.

The minimum age for using a temporarily imported motorcycle of up to 125 cc (without a passeger) is 16 years; to carry a passenger or to use a motorcycle over 125 cc, the minimum age is 18 years; and motorcycles of over 350 cc may not be used by anyone under 21 years of age. Motorcycles of less than 150 cc capacity may not be used on motorways. No motorcycle may tow a trailer. Crash helmets are compulsory.

Motorcycles

In 1988 Italy was one of the last two countries in Europe to make the wearing of seat belts compulsory.
From 26 April 1990 children between the ages of 4 and 10 years, seated in the front or rear of a car, must use a restraint system.

Seat belts,
children in cars

Traffic on main roads has priority where the road is marked with the priority sign (a square with the corner pointing downwards, coloured white with a red border or yellow with a black and white border). Otherwise (even on roundabouts) the rule is 'right before left' motorists give precedence to vehicles coming from their right. On narrow mountain roads traffic going up has priority, as do most other public service vehicles. Postal buses also have right of way, their routes are marked by a special sign. If two vehicles are travelling in opposite directions and the drivers of each vehicle want to turn left, they must pass in front of each other (not drive round as in Britain).

Priority

The directions of the traffic police (polizia stradale) should be strictly observed. Fines for traffic offences are high.

Traffic police

A change of lane both before and after overtaking must be signalled with the direction indicators; in addition, outside built-up areas the horn must also be sounded during daylight. After dark headlamps must be flashed for the same purpose.

Overtaking

Practical Information

Prohibition of use of horn

In towns the use of the horn is frequently prohibited, either by an appropriate road sign, (a horn with a stroke through it) or by the legend "Zona di silenzio".

Lights

On well-lit roads sidelights only may be used (except in tunnels and galleries where dipped headlights must be used at all times).

Drinking and driving

There are heavy penalties for driving under the influence of alcohol.

Parking

The "Rimozione forzata" (compulsory towing-away service) tows away illegally parked vehicles. A visitor who fails to find his vehicle in the place where he has parked it should apply either to the town police (vigili urbani) or direct to the depot of towed-away vehicles (Parco Auto Requisite, Via Circondaria 16, tel. 35 15 62).

Accidents

In the event of an accident make sure that you have all the necessary particulars and supporting evidence (statements by witnesses, sketches, photographs, etc.). If the accident involves personal injury it must be reported to the police. You should notify your own insurance company as soon as possible, and if you are responsible or partly responsible for the accident you should also inform the Italian insurance company or bureau whose address is given on your green card. This agency will give advice and supply the name of a lawyer should the foreign driver be subject to penal proceedings. – If your car is a total write-off the Italian customs authorities must be informed at once; otherwise you might be required to pay the full import duty on the vehicle.

Breakdown assistance

In case of breakdown on any Italian road dial 116 at the nearest telephone box or if on a motorway use the emergency telephones positioned every 1¼ miles (2 km). Tell the operator where you are, registration number and type of car and the nearest ACI office will be informed for immediate asssistance. Towing from the breakdown location to the nearest ACI affiliated garage is free but a charge is made if the vehicle is towed anywhere else, and any additional service must be paid for.

Warning triangle

The use of a warning triangle is compulsory in the event of an accident or breakdown and must be placed on the road not less than 55 yards (50 metres) behind the vehicle; motorists failing to comply may be fined.

Museums

Warning

Since the opening times of museums in Italy frequently change it is not possible to give up-to-date information. Visitors should therefore make enquiries before going to a particular museum.

List of museums

Appartamenti ex Reali (former royal apartments)
See A–Z, Palazzo Pitti

Casa Buonarotti (Michelangelo Museum)
See A–Z, Casa Buonarroti

Casa e Museo di Dante (Dante Museum)
See A–Z, Casa di Dante

Collezione Contini-Bonacossi
Palazina della Meridiana (Giardino di Boboli, (Entrance through
Galleria d'Arte Moderna in the Palazzo Pitti)
Open: Tues., Thurs. and Sat. 9 a.m.–noon
Visits only by prior arrangement
(Segreteria degli Uffizi, tel. 21 83 41)

Conservatorio Musicale Luigi Cherubini
See A–Z, Conservatorio Musicale Luigi Cherubini

Gipsoteca dell'Instituto d'Arte
Piazzale di Porta Romana 9
Visits by prior arrangement (tel. 22 05 21)

Museo dell'Antica Casa Fiorentina (Museo Davanzati)
See A–Z, Pallazzo Davanzati

Museo Archeologico Centrale dell'Etruria (Archaeological
Museum)
See A–Z, Museo Archeologico Centrale dell'Etruria

Museo degli Agenti (Silver Museum)
See A–Z, Pallazzo Pitti

Museo Bardini e Galleria Corsi
See A–Z, Museo Bardini

Museo del Bigallo
See A–Z, Monastero del Bigallo

Museo Botanico
See A–Z, Orto Botanico

Museo delle Carrozze (Coach Museum)
See A–Z, Palazzo Pitti

Museo di Firenze Com'era
See A–Z, Museo Storico Topografico

Museo della Fondazione Horne
See A–Z, Museo della Fondazione Horne

Museo di Geologia e Paleontologia dell'Università
Via La Pira 4
Open Mon. 2–6 p.m., Tues., Wed., Thurs., Sat. 9 a.m.–1 p.m. and
first Sun. in month, 9.30 a.m.–12.30 p.m. Admission free

Museo dei Gessi (Plaster Museum)
Piazzale di Porta Romana 9
Visits by prior arrangement: tel. 22 05 21

Museo Mediceo (Medici Museum)
See A–Z, Palazzo Medici Riccardi

Museo di Mineralogia e Litologia dell'Università
Via La Pira 4
Open 9 a.m.–1 p.m., Wed. also 3–6 p.m. and first Sun. in month
9.30 a.m.–12.30 p.m. Admission free.

Museo Nazionale di Antropologia ed Etnologia
(Museum of Folk Art)
See A–Z, Palazzo Nonfinito

Museo Nazionale del Bargello
See A–Z, Palazzo Bargello

Museo dell'Opera del Duomo (Museo di Santa Maria del Fiore)
See A–Z, Museo dell'Opera del Duomo

Museo dell'Opera di Santa Croce
See A–Z, Santa Croce

Museo delle Porcellane
See A–Z, Giardino di Boboli

Museo di Preistoria
Via S. Egidio 21
Open Mon.–Sat. 9.30 a.m.–12.30 p.m.; closed Sun., public
holidays. Admission free.

Museo di San Marco
See A–Z, San Marco

Museo di Santa Maria del Fiore
(cathedral museum)
See A–Z, Museo dell'Opera del Duomo

Museo Stibbert
See A–Z, Museo Stibbart

Museo (e Istituto) di Storia della Scienza
(History of Science)
See A–Z, Palazzo Castellani

Museo Storico Topografico "Firenze com'era"
("Florence as it used to be")
See A–Z, Museo Storico Topografico

Museo degli Strumenti Musicali Antichi
See A–Z, Conservatorio Musicale
Luigi Cherubini

Museo del Tempio Israelitico (Jewish museum)
Via Farini 4
Visits only by prior arrangement: tel. 24 52 52

Museo Zoologico "La Specoloa"
See A–Z, Museo Zoologico

Opificio e Museo delle Pietre Dure
(Mosaic Museum)
See A–Z, Opificio e Museo delle Pietre Dure

Opening times

Shops	Summer 9 a.m.–1 p.m., 4–7.30 p.m. (many food shops open at 8 a.m.) Closed Sat. afternoon.
	Winter 9 a.m.–12.30, 3.30–7.30 p.m. Closed Mon. morning.
Chemists	Summer Mon.–Fri. 8.30 a.m.–12.30, 4–8 p.m. Winter mon.–Fri. 8.30 a.m.–12.30, 3.30–7.30 p.m.

Open Mon.–Fri. 8.30 a.m.–1.30 or 2.30 p.m. Some banks are open for an hour in the afternoon, usually 3–4 p.m. — Banks

Open Mon.–Fri. 8.30 a.m.–2 p.m., Sat 8.30 a.m.–noon — Post offices

The opening times are given under the entry for each museum (see A–Z and Practical Information, Museums). It should be borne in mind that most museums are closed on public holidays in addition to the normal "rest day", often a Monday.
In addition there are often closures as a result of staff shortages, strikes, renovation, etc. and it is advisable before visiting a museum to check that it will be open. — Museums

The larger churches are usually open from the morning until noon and for the most part also from 4 or 5 p.m. until dusk; some of the major churches are open all day. It is possible to see the interior of a church during a service if care is taken to avoid disturbing the worshippers. — Churches

Petrol

See Gasoline

Police

tel. 113 — Emergency

Police Headquarters, Via Zara 2, tel. 4 97 71 — Questura

Borgognissanti 48, tel. 112 — Carabinieri

Municipal police, Piazzale della Porta al Prato 6, tel. 35 21 41 — Vigili urbani

Traffic police, tel. 57 77 77 — Polizia stradale

Railway police, tel. 21 22 96 — Polizia Ferroviaria

Postal services (Posta)

Letters within Italy and to EC countries (up to 20 grams) 750 lire Postcards 550 lire — Postal rates

In Italy letter boxes are painted red. — Letter boxes

Post offices are usually open on Mon.–Fri. 8.30 a.m.–2 p.m., Sat. 8.30 a.m. –noon; the main post office in the Via Pellicceria, tel. 21 41 45, is open from 8.15 a.m.–7.30 p.m.; telegraph and telephone services are available day and night. — Post offices

Stamps can be bought at post offices, at tobacconists (indicated by a large T above the door) and from stamp machines. — Stamps

Public Holidays

Shops, offices and schools are closed on these days.

1 January (New Year's Day); 6 January (Epiphany); Easter; 25 April (Liberation Day, 1945).

1 May (Labour Day); 1st Sunday in June (Proclamation of the Republic).

15 August (Assumption: a family celebration, the high point of the Italian summer holiday migration).

1 November (All Saints); 1st Sunday in November (Day of National Unity); 8 December (Immaculate Conception).

25 and 26 December (Christmas).

In addition, 24 June is a feast day in honor of Florence's patron saint (St John the Baptist), when shops and offices normally remain open.

Public transport

Buses

Buses are the only form of public transport in Florence. Tickets are bought from officially authorised sales points or from tobacconists.

Information

Excursions in the vicinity of Florence can be made using the buses of the SITA organisation. Details of departures and arrivals are available through a computerised service in four languages at the bus station (Via S. Caterina da Siena 15r, near the rail station).

ATAF

Public transport headquarters ATAF (Azienda Trasporti Auto-linee Fiorentine); for information tel. 58 05 28.

Radio

During the tourist season the Italian radio service RAI broadcasts programmes for foreign visitors (news, commentaries, etc.) in various languages.
Radio Uno O.M. (medium wave) transmits daily at 1.56 p.m. the programme Green Wave–Euroradio in four languages (messages for tourists and traffic conditions). Emergency messages to tourists are also broadcast in English and Italian at various times throughout the day.
Further information can be obtained from the automobile clubs or the police.

Railroad stations

The main railroad station for national and international passenger traffic is:

Information

Stazione Centrale Santa Maria Novella
tel. 27 87 85 (8 a.m.–8 p.m.)

Lost property

(Ufficio Oggetti Rinvenuti): head office, tel. 27 67.

Railway police

Polizia Ferroviaria, tel. 21 22 96

Accommodation service

Consorzio I.T.A., tel. 28 28 93 (9 a.m.–8.30 p.m.)

Florence, main railway station

Rail services

The Italian railroad system has a total length of 10,000 miles (16,000 km). Most of it is run by the Italian State Railroad (Ferrovie dello Stato – FS).

Ferrovie dello Stato (FS)

Information about rail services, and the concessionary fares available, can be obtained from the Italian State Tourist Office or from Italian State Railroad offices abroad:

50 Conduit Street, London SW1, tel. (01) 434 3844

United Kingdom

765 Route 83, Suite 105, Chicago, Ill.
5670 Wilshire Boulevard, Los Angeles, Cal.
668 Fifth Avenue, New York, NY.

United States of America

2055 Peel Street, Suite 102, Montreal
111 Richmond Street West, Suite 419, Toronto

Canada

Stazione Centrale Santa Maria Novella, tel.: 27 87 85

In Florence

Italian rail tickets have limited validity; this depends on the length of the journey, from one day for journeys up to 155 miles (250 km) to six days for journeys of more than 620 miles (1000 km). For day return tickets covering a maximum distance of 31 miles (50 km), and for three-day return tickets covering a maximum distance of 155 miles (250 km) there is a 15 per cent discount.

Tickets

Practical Information

Children

Children accompanied by an adult travel free up to the age of 4; between 4 and 12 they pay half fare.

Tourist card

The Tourist Card or Biglietto Turistico Liberia Circolazione (BTLC) is valid in first or second class for an unlimited number of journeys on the entire Italian rail network for periods of 8, 15, 21 or 30 days. A second-class ticket valid for 8 days costs $115 (£72), and for 30 days $200 (£125), First-class fares are $180 (£115) for 8 days and $320 (£200) for 30 days. These figures are approximate. The card is sold abroad by FS recognised agencies and in Italy at mainline stations.

"Kilometric Card"

With a kilometric (chilometrico) card up to five persons can make various individual journeys (maximum 20) with a total length of 1864 miles (3000 km). The kilometric card costs approximately $160 (£107) in first class and $90 (£60) in second class.

Restaurants (Ristorante)

Notice

Every restaurant must hand the customer a receipted bill; this must be shown on demand to a tax inspector in the vicinity of the restaurant. Failure to do so may invoke a fine.

Customers must always be on guard against being overcharged or served with something which they have not ordered. This happens especially with fish restaurants. If you are surprised at the price on the bill which does not accord with that on the menu, you may be told that you have been served with a particularly large lobster, etc. If this has not been ordered, do not hesitate to resist and if necessary send for the police.

In addition to the often relatively expensive and lavish "ristorante" there are in Italy many usually modest but good-quality establishments called "osteria" (originally a country inn where wine and simple dishes are served) and "trattoria" (an urban variant of an osteria, generally serving typical regional food). If you are in a hurry to get something to eat, you should look for a "pizzeria" or patronise a "tavola calda" or a "rosticceria" (both resembling a cafetaria).

Ristorante

*Enocteca Pinchiorri, Via Ghibellina 87; tel. 24 27 77
 (an elegant restaurant in a 16th c. palace; nouvelle cuisine).
*Sabatini, Via de' Panzani 9a; tel.28 28 02
 (a traditional luxury restaurant).
Buca Lapi, Via del Trebbio 1r; tel. 21 37 68
 (characteristic middle-range inn).
Cavallino, Via delle Farine 6r; tel. 21 58 18
 (meals served in the open air in summer).
Dino, Via Ghibellina 51r; tel. 24 14 52
 (modern middle-range restaurant with an extensive menu).
Don Chisciotte, Via Cosimo Ridolfi 4/6r; tel. 47 54 30
 (elegant restaurant).
Enoteca Pane e Vino, Via Poggio Bracciolini 48; tel. 68 37 46
 (typical Florentine restaurant, excellent wine list).
Giglio Rosso, Via Panzani 35r; tel. 21 17 95
Il Coccodrillo, Via della Scala 5; tel. 28 36 22
 (Tuscan and international cuisine).

La Capannina di Sante, Piazza Ravenna; tel. 68 83 45
   (typical relatively expensive Tuscan restaurant in a wooden
   house by the Arno; many fish dishes).
La Greppia, Lungarno Ferrucci 8; tel. 6 81 23 41
   (rustic restaurant with a terrace).
La Vecchia Cucina, Viale de Amicis 1r; tel. 67 21 43
   (high-class restaurant; menu varies according to season).
Lo Strettoio, Via di Serpiolle 7; tel. 40 30 44
   (inn housed in a 17th c. villa; terrace with view of Florence;
   imaginative cuisine).

Coco Lezzone, Via dei Parioncino 26r; tel. 28 71 78   Osterie
   (pleasant restaurant in Tuscan style; good Tuscan cuisine).
Guiseppe Alessi, Via di Mazzo 24/25r; tel. 24 18 21
   (good Tuscan cuisine, relatively moderately priced).
Pepolino, Via Franceschi Furrucci 16r; tel. 60 89 05
   (pleasant inn; specialities are offal and fish dishes).

Antico Fattore, Via Lambertesca 1; tel. 26 12 15   Trattorie
Baldini, Via il Prato 96r; tel. 28 76 63
Bordino, Via Stracciatella 9r; tel. 21 30 48
   (characteristic inn; moderate prices).
Buca Mario, Piazza Ottaviani 16r; tel. 21 41 79
   (typical Florentine trattoria).
Cammillo, Borgo Sant' Jacopo 57r; tel. 21 24 27
   (typical Florentine trattoria, but rather expensive).
Del Carmine, Piazza del Carmine 18r; tel. 21 86 01
San Zanobi, Via San Zanobi 33r; tel. 47 52 86
   (excellent stuffed calamari; good Chianti wines).
Sostanza detto "Il Troia", Via del Porcellana 25r; tel. 21 26 91
   (Florentine inn; offal and their own Chianti are recom-
   mended).
Vittoria, Via della Fondoria 52; tel. 22 56 57
   (known for its fish dishes).

China Town, Via Vecchietti 6–10r; tel. 29 44 70   Chinese restaurants
Grande Cina, Via dei Castellani 18/24r; tel. 21 57 50
Hong Kong, Piazza dell 'Olio 10r; tel. 21 20 90
Il Mandarino, Via Condotta 17r; tel. 29 61 30
La Grande Miraglia, Via Ponte alle Mosse 9r; tel. 35 63 01

Giapponese, Via dei Neri 72r; tel. 21 09 40   Japanese restaurant

Shopping

Streets where there are many antique shops are: Borgo Ogni-   Antiques
santi, Via Maggio, Via Fossi, Via di Santo Spirito and Via delle
Vigna Nuova.

The majority of the book shops are to be found in the Santa   Books
Croce district.

Many shops in Via Calzauioli, Via Tornabuoni, Via Strozzi and   Clothing and lingerie
Via de'Guicciardini sell clothing and lingerie. For lace and knit-
wear visitors should try the shops in Via Calimala, in the Piazza
della Repubblica and in Via Por Santa Maria. The firm of "Lisio"
in Via dei Fossi specialises in valuable brocades and silks.

Souvenirs and pictures on sale in the arcades of the Palazzo degli Uffizi

Florence also has its mobile bookshops

Florence is famous for its leather goods. In the Piazza Santa Croce, in the Piazza San Lorenzo and in Via Calzaiuoli there are many shops selling a wide selection of clothing and accessories in leather. Among the leading firms are "Ciocca Rosina" (Via Calzaiuoli 76r), "Bottega Veneta" (Piazza Ognisanti 3/4r) and "Marsupio" (Via Pistoiese 136), "Il Bisonte" (Via del Parione 25a/r) sells very beautiful handbags. There are very many shoe shops in the Piazza della Repubblica, in Via Calzaiuoli and Via Tornabuoni. "Beltrami" (Via Calzaiuoli 44r) offers a very representative selection.

Leather goods

Yet Florence is not only the town of leather goods, but also the town of jewelry. Beautifully crafted items of gold and silver can be found in particular on the Ponto Vecchio.

Jewelry

Wine is, of course, something which many visitors take home from Florence. If the visitor would like to see a comprehensive selection of what is on offer he should go to the "Enoteca Bonatti" in Via Gioberti or the "Enoteca Internazionale de Rham" in the Piazza S.S. Annunziata.

Wine

See separate entry

Markets

Uppim Via Statuto 19
        Viale Talenti
        Via Gioberti
        Via Speziali
Standa Piazza Dalmazia 12/14
        Via Petrapiana 42/44
        Viale Mille 140

Department stores

See separate entry

Opening times

In Italy value added tax is up to 38%. On leaving the country tourists can recover this tax on presentation of the relevant receipts (see "Fiscal receipt" below). To avoid delays at the frontiers visitors can make use of the firm "Tax Free Shop for Tourist" (branches at 15 frontier points and at several airports).

Value added tax

In Italy the law demands that a numbered fiscal receipt (rice-vuta fiscale) is issued after paying for a wide range of goods and services, including meals and accommodation. The receipt shows the total cost including value added tax. Tourists should ensure this receipt is issued as they can be fined along with the supplier if the receipt cannot be produced.

Fiscal receipt

Sightseeing

Information on organized sightseeing tours can be obtained from the Italian State Tourist Offices (see Tourist Information, p. 169).

For an individual sightseeing tour a guide can be hired through "Ufficio Guide Turistiche", Viale Gramsci, 9a, tel. 2 47 81 88.

Authorized guides

Half day for 1–17 persons   Lire 73,000
Each additional person   Lire 1,650

Charges

"The Florence Experience", a film show lasting 45 minutes, provides visitors with a general impression of Florence and its history. The sound-track is in six languages. Performances take place every hour on the hour: June to August daily from 10 a.m.– 10 p.m.; September to May Mon.–Fri. 9 a.m.–5 p.m., Sat. and Sun. 9 a.m.–3 p.m.

Multivision show

Sports facilities

Stadium	Stadio Comunale Viale Manfredo Fanti Stadium (55,000 seats), swimming pool
Race-courses	Galoppo Ippodromo del Visarno Trotto Ippodromo delle Muline Cascine, see A–Z, Cascine
Golf	Golf dell'Ugolino Grassina, Strada Chiatigiana 3 (7·5 miles – 12 km out of Florence)
Tennis	Circolo del Tennis, Cascine, Viale Viscarno 1 Club Sportivo Firenze Via Fosso Macinante 13
Open-air swimming baths	Piscina Comunale Bellariva, Lungarno Colombo 6 Piscina Costoli, Viale Paoli Piscine Poggetto, Via Michele Marcati 24b Piscina Le Pavionere, Via delle Cascine

Taxi

Radio taxis	Via Steccuto 12; tel. 43 90 Via Valdinievole 44c; tel. 47 98
Taxi ranks	Taxi ranks are listed, together with their telephone numbers and a map, in the front of the classified telephone directory (Pagine Gialle).

Telephone

International dialing code from Florence	To the United Kingdom: 00 44 To the United States: 00 1 To Canada: 00 1
International dailing code to Florence	From the United Kingdom: 010 39 55 From the United States: 011 39 55 From Canada: 011 39 55
	In dailing an international call the initial zero of the local dailing code should be omitted.
Pay phones	Public telephones function both with 200 lire gettoni (telephone tokens) and 100 or 200 lire coins, or 500 lire coins in the new payphones. Since international calls need a considerable supply of coins, it is more convenient to find a telephone which will accept telephone credit cards; these are obtainable from the SIP (the state telephone company). There are also telephone boxes in most bars, from which local calls can be made. These bars have a yellow sign outside; if the sign has "teleselezione" or "interurbana" on it then international calls can be dialed direct.
Post office	In addition calls can be made from post offices and the telephone office of the SIP (there is one in the main station).

To make a call, insert payment *before* lifting the receiver; the dailing tone consists of short and long sounds.

Making calls

A cheap rate operates on Sundays and public holidays, as well as from 1 p.m. on Saturdays and other days immediately preceding a public holiday, and between 10 p.m. and 8 a.m. daily.

Cheap rate

Theaters, Concerts

Teatro Comunale
Corso Italia 12
tel. 2 77 91

Opera, concerts

Teatro della Pergola
Via della Pergola 18
tel. 2 47 96 51

Sala Bianca
Piazza Pitti

Concerts

Sala del Conservatorio di Musica
Piazza Bella Arti 2

Teatro del Oriuolo
Via dell'Oriuolo
tel. 2 34 05 07

Plays

Teatro Verdi
Via Ghibellina 99
tel. 29 62 42

Revue

Especially in the summer numerous cultural events take place in Florence. (See Events.)

Theatrical and musical festivals

Time

Italy observes Central European Time (one hour ahead of Greenwich Mean Time; six hours ahead of New York Time). From the end of March to the end of September summer time (two hours ahead of GMT; seven hours ahead of New York time) is in force.

Tipping (Mancia)

In hotels and restaurants the service charge is included, but gratuities of 5–10% of the amount of the bill are still expected. In "bars" and Italian cafés service is often not included and in this case 12–15% is normal. Taxi fares are usually rounded up by the passenger, porters expect 2000 lire for each piece of luggage carried. In Italy it is not customary to tip chambermaids or hairdressers. Usherettes taking you to your seat in cinemas and theaters should also be tipped.

Tourist information

The first place to go for information when you are planning a trip to Florence is the Italian State Tourist Office (ENIT).

Practical Information

<table>
<tr><td>United Kingdom</td><td>1 Princes Street, London W1R 8AY,
tel. (071) 408–1254</td></tr>
<tr><td>United States of America</td><td>500 North Michigan Avenue, Chicago, IL 60611;
tel. (312) 644 0990–1
630 Fifth Avenue, Suite 1565, New York, NY 10111;
tel. (212) 245 4822–4
360 Post Street, Suite 801, San Francisco, CA 94108;
tel. (415) 392 6206–7</td></tr>
<tr><td>Canada</td><td>c/o Alitalia, 85 Richmond Street, Toronto;
tel. (416) 36–31–348</td></tr>
<tr><td>In Florence</td><td>Ufficio Informazioni Turistiche dell'Ente Provinciale per il Turismo
Via Manzoni 16, tel. 24 78 141
Open Mon.–Fri. 8.30 a.m.–1.30 p.m., 4–6.30 p.m.;
Sat. 8.30 a.m.–1.30 p.m.

Ufficio Informazioni Turistiche dell'Azienda Autonoma di Turismo
Via Tornabuoni 15; Tel. 217 459
Open Mon.–Sat. 8 a.m.–2 p.m.</td></tr>
<tr><td>Telephone information</td><td>By telephoning 116 information and advice can be obtained in the whole of Italy (multi-lingual personnel).</td></tr>
</table>

Tours of the city

<table>
<tr><td>Note</td><td>The following suggested sightseeing programme is meant to help the first-time visitor to Florence to get the best from his stay. Buildings, squares, monuments, etc. which are featured in the A–Z section are printed in **bold** type.</td></tr>
<tr><td>One day</td><td>A first impression of the magnificent situation and the many fine buildings of the city can be obtained from the **Piazzale Michelangelo**, from where there is the best view of the metropolis of the Arno. From here it is easy to identify the most celebrated sights and to reach them. Another fine view can be enjoyed from the Church of **San Miniato al Monte** above the Piazzale Michelangelo.
When you have seen enough of the beauties of Florence from a distance you will want to make a tour of the city. (The following sightseeing tour can be easily made with the help of the plan at the end of this guide.)
A good starting point is the **Piazza di Santa Maria Novella** near the station. On the north side of this lively square stands the Church of **Santa Maria Novella**, one of the most famous Florentine churches; on the south side extends the **Loggia di San Paolo**. North-east of the Piazza di Santa Maria Novella is **San Lorenzo**. Both the Church of St Laurence as well as the Lorentian Library and the Medici Chapels are architectural masterpieces of the highest rank. Obliquely opposite the Church of San Lorenzo rises the mighty building of the **Palazzo Medici-Riccardi**. Three hundred metres south of the Via Camillo and the Via Martelli you reach the **Piazza del Duomo**. This square and the Piazza San Giovanni are bordered by the **Duomo Santa Maria del Fiore**, the dome of which is the landmark of Florence, the **Battistero San Giovanni**, the **Palazzo Arcivescovile**, the</td></tr>
</table>

Loggia del Bigallo, the Palzzo Guadagni and the **Museo dell'Opera del Duomo**. Passing along the Via Calzaiuoli, one of the principal shopping streets of the city, you reach the 14th c. Church of **Orsanmichele**. Further east in the Piazza San Firenze your attention is drawn to the Church of **Badia Fiorentina**, the **Palazzo del Bargello**, which houses the National Museum containing sculptures by the most important Tuscan masters of the 14th–16th c., the **Palazzo Gondi** and the Church of **San Firenze**. Still further east on the far side of the Piazza Santa Croce rises the Franciscan Church **Santa Croce**, one of the most beautiful buildings in Italy. Passing the **Biblioteca Nazionale Centrale** you arrive at the bank of the Arno and follow it in a westerly direction to the picturesque **Ponte Vecchio**. From here it is only a few steps to the **Piazza della Signoria**, which together with the **Palazzo Vecchio**, the **Palazzo degli Uffizi** and the **Loggia dei Lanzi** which are among the principal sights of the city. The tour continues through the **Loggia Mercato Nuova** where numerous craftworkers ply their trade, as far as the Piazza and the **Palazzo Davanzati**. No less impressive are the **Palazzo Spini-Ferroni** and opposite this the Church of **Santa Trinita** on the bank of the Arno. Passing along the elegant **Via Tornabuoni** you reach the **Palazzo Strozzi**, considered to be one of the finest Renaissance palaces of Florence. Having then admired the nearby **Palazzo Rucellai** you arrive a few minutes later once more at the Piazza di Santa Maria Novella, the start and finish of the tour of the town.

If you still have time and the sightseeing tour has not taken your whole day then a visit in the afternoon to the **Palazzo degli Uffizi** and the **Galleria degli Uffizi** are almost obligatory. (Since opening times are often altered you should make sure before your visit that the picture gallery is open until the evening.)
Highly recommended is the multivision show "the Florence Experience" (see Practical Information, Sightseeing; performances in the summer until 10 p.m.).

Two days

If you have another day at your disposal you might well spend the second morning visiting the **Palazzo Pitti** on the south bank of the Arno. A visit to the picture gallery, the Royal Apartments and the other museums housed in the palace is one of the highlights of a visit to Florence. Afterwards you should not fail to see the **Giardino di Boboli**. A walk through this extensive park brings you to the **Forte del Belvedere**, from where there is another excellent view of Florence.
The afternoon is reserved for a tour of the northern part of the inner city. Noteworthy here are the Church and Museum of **San Marco** (museum open only until 2 p.m.). After this you proceed in a southerly direction past the university buildings to the Church of **Santissima Annunziata**. The ground plan of the church and convent are an irregular architectural masterpiece; the church houses unique art treasures. Opposite the church extends the **Piazza della Santissima Annunziata** with the important buildings of the **Spedale degli Innocenti** and the **Palazzo Riccardi-Manelli**. In the evening you can enjoy a visit to a concert or a ballet performance – in summer there is a large choice of cultural activities (see Practical Information, Events, Theatres, Concerts).

Three days

Almost as famous as the picture gallery of the Uffizi is the art collection of the **Galleria dell'Accademia**. No less interesting is a visit to the Church of **Santa Spirito**, within which are art treasures of immeasurable worth, or perhaps you would like to visit the **Casa Buonarroti**, in which are a number of exhibits commemorating the life and works of Michelangelo.

A trip in the afternoon to **Fiesole** will be a contrast. This little town, barely 6 miles/10 km north-east of Florence, is well worth a visit, not only for its interesting features but also because from here there is a magnificent panorama of Florence.

Travel documents

Passport

British and US citizens require only a passport (or the one-year British visitor's passport). This applies also to citizens of Canada, Ireland and many other countries.

If you lose your passport a substitute document can be issued by the British, US, Canadian, etc. consulate. It is a good idea to photocopy or note down the main particulars (number, date, etc.) of your passport, so that in case of loss you can give the necessary details to the police.

Driving licence, etc.

British (green coloured), US and other national driving licences are valid in Italy, but must be accompanied by an Italian translation (obtainable free of charge from automobile clubs). The "pink" EC type licence does not require a translation. Motorists should also take the registration document of their car.

Green card

See Insurance, p. 152.

Nationality plate

Foreign cars must display the oval nationality plate.

When to go

From April to June and from September to October, when the average temperature lies between 15° and 20° C, are the best periods for a visit to Florence. However, it is advisable to avoid Easter and Whitsun, when the city becomes so crowded that sightseeing is far from enjoyable. In July and August it is often difficult to find hotel accommodation; apart from foreign visitors it appears as if the whole of Italy is on the move!

The quietest time is from November to March, when many visitors are prepared to accept the risk of unsettled weather.

Climate Table Months	Temperature in °C		Hours of sunshine per day	Rainy days	Rainfall in mm
	Average maximum	Average minimum			
January	8·7	2·1	4·0	7·0	60·5
February	10·5	2·7	4·5	7·0	58·0
March	14·3	5·4	5·2	9·0	72·5
April	18·0	8·3	6·8	8·0	66·5
May	23·3	12·1	8·8	7·5	61·0
June	27·5	15·6	9·3	6·5	69·5
July	30·3	18·0	10·7	3·0	25·5
August	30·2	18·0	9·4	3·5	35·5
September	25·6	15·0	7·5	5·5	68·5
October	19·6	11·0	6·0	8·5	97·0
November	13·6	6·5	3·5	9·5	101·5
December	10·0	3·8	3·0	9·0	78·0
Year	19·3	9·8	6·7 (2488)	84	795

Wine

From time immemorial Italy has been a producer of wine; today its total production is greater than anywhere else (almost a quarter of the wine production in the world comes from Italy). Tuscany is one of the best organised wine producing regions of the country.

General

From Tuscany comes one of the best known wines in the world, Chianti. It is made from the dark Sangiovese grape together with Canaiolo and paler Trebbiano and Malvasia grapes. Chianti colli Fiorentini, produced in the immediate vicinity of Florence, is a fresh ruby-red wine which is excellent as a table wine. Chianto Classico comes from the area between Florence and Siena; this soft slightly bitter wine is generally at its best between two and five years old, but it can last for a decade. 'Classic' Chianti can be recognised by the black cockerel on the label, and Chianto Putto, which has a little angel as its motif, is no less inferior in quality. The fact that the wine producers of Chianti have recently met with increasing sales resistance may be attributed to there being considerable differences in quality. Mass production, especially outside the actual heart of the Chianti region, has led to many varieties being unpopular with connoisseurs.

Red wines

An excellent red wine which, however, is rather expensive, is Brunello di Montalcino. Good years age excellently and as they do so they develop an elegant bouquet. From the same region comes Rosso dei Vigneti di Brunello, prepared from the same kind but younger grapes. It is dry and velvety, has a rich bouquet and is drunk young.

Also excellent is Vino Nobile di Motepulciano from south-east Tuscany. The colour is brick – or pomegranate – red, and the wine is dry with a light bouquet of violets. Only the very best years are laid down to mature.

Growing demand has led to the resurgence of Tuscan white wines. Although only red wine can officially be sold under the name of "Chianti", nevertheless an increasing amount of white Chianti from the Trabbiano and Malvasia grapes is produced in this area. These wines are generally dry and white, and with suitable handling can also be fruity. They are marketed under a variety of names. Above average quality is Galestro, which has a maximum alcohol content of 10.5% and is dry, fresh and fruity. Bianco della Lega is similar. One of the best Tuscan white wines is Monte Carlo, produced east of Lucca. It is prepared from various varieties of grape and depending on the producer has differing qualities. In general it is drunk young. A white wine with a tradition is Vernaccia di San Gimignano. According to whether it is prepared from clear must or from must including the skins, it is light, fresh and with a flowery bouquet, or rich and dark in colour. This wine, too, is seldom kept for long.

White wines

Those who prefer a rosé are recommended to try Brolio Rosé; it is a very light wine as is Rosé di Bolgheri which is made from Sangiovese and Canaiolo grapes.

Rosé wines

it is difficult to discover the particular kinds of Italian wines from the names usually found on the wine labels. The names can refer to places or types of grape, but are often pure inventions or brand names. It is not at all unusual for red and white wines with very different attributes to be found under the same name.

Wine labels

The Italian wine regulations of 1963 established three grades of quality:

"Denominazione Semplice", the lowest grade, designates table wine; a definite quality is not prescribed.

"Denominazione di Origine Controllata" (DOC) is the next grade. Every firm can apply for their wines to be registered as DOC. DOC wines must originate from an officially recognised area of production; they must be made from specific kinds of grapes and prepared according to approved methods. The details for each DOC area and producers are laid down. DOC wines are subjected to testing and in addition to their own label must be provided with a DOC label.

The highest grade, "Denominazione di Origine Controllata e Garantita" (DOCG), is only given to the chiocest wines of individual producers. The wine must be bottled by the producer or other responsible people and the original bottling must be guaranteed by an official seal.

Language of
the wine label

Amabile	delicate
Annata	year
Azienda agricola (agraria)	estate
Barbera	full-bodied grape variety from Piedmont
Bianco	white
Cantina	wine cellar
Cantina sociale	vintners' co-operative
Classico	from the centre and best area of the region
Frizzante	lightly sparkling
Graddazione alcoolica	alcohol content
Metodo champenois	fermented in the bottle
Nero	dark red
Riserva	wine laid down for an officially approved time (generally 3 years)
Rosato	rosé
Rosso	red
Secco	dry
Spumante	sparkling
Superiore	designation of DOC wines of superior quality
Tenementi	property or estate
Uva	grape
Vendemmia	vintage (year)
Vigna	vineyard
Vilo ordinario	ordinary wine (non estate bottled)
Vino di tavola	table wine

Youth hostels

Ostello Santa Monaca
Via Santa Monaca 6, tel. 26 83 38

Villa Camerata
Viale Righi 2/4, tel. 60 14 51

Villa Favard
Via Rocca Tedalda; tel. 69 08 47
(in summer sleeping in the open is free)

The Wines of Tuscany

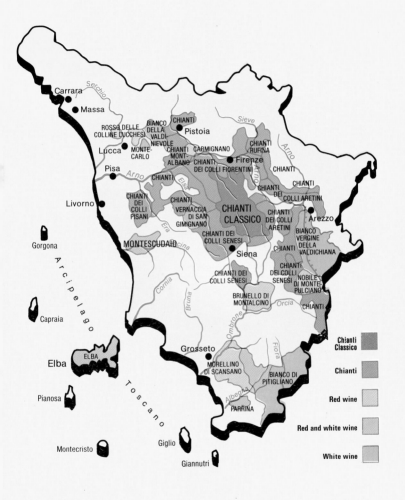

Chianti Classico

Chianti

Red wine

Red and white wine

White wine

Useful Telephone Numbers at a Glance

General emergency number	113
Emergency calls	
Ambulance (Pronto Soccorso Autoambulanze)	21 22 22
Breakdown assistance (Automobile Club d'Italia, ACI)	116
Fire Department (Vigili del Fuoco)	115
Medical emergencies (Guardia Medica; 24 hours)	47 78 91
First-aid (Misericordia)	21 22 22
Police:	
Criminal police (Carabinieri)	112
Municipal police (Vigili Urbani)	35 21 41
Railway police	21 22 96
Traffic police (Polizia stradale)	57 77 77
Information	
General (multi-lingual personnel)	116
Automobile Club d'Italia (ACI)	2 48 61
Italian State Tourist Office (ENIT):	
London	*(071) 408 1254
Chicago	(312) 644 0990–1
New York	(212) 245 4822–4
San Francisco	(415) 392 6206–7
Florence:	
News service (by telephone)	190
Public Transport (ATAF)	5 31 91
Road conditions	194
Tourist office (ENIT)	24 78 141
Train information	27 87 85
Weather forecast for Tuscany	19 11
Lost property	
Municipal lost property office	36 79 43
Railway lost property office	27 67
Taxi (Radio)	43 90 and 47 98
Telephone	
Information for call within Italy	12
Information for international calls	184
Operator for international calls	15 or 170
Dialing codes:	
from the United Kingdom to Florence	010 39 55
from the United States and Canada to Florence	011 39 55
from Florence to the United Kingdom	00 44
from Florence to the United States and Canada	00 1

* (01) 408 1254 until 6 May 1990